The Truth Between the Lines: From *History* to *Our* Story, and Beyond
A critique of American society and the African-American community

By Akhee Jamiel Hassan Williams

2

To my family, always loving, never judging, always teaching, sometimes preaching. There through thick and thin, the good and the bad. I am so grateful. These bonds cannot be broken.

To my friends and colleagues, thank you so very much. Thank you for all your smiles and hugs, your support and encouragement, your sincerity and warmth.

To my Love. You improve me.

Love, appreciation, and respect to you all.

4

"Let me say, at the risk of appearing ridiculous, that the true revolutionary is guided by strong feelings of love."

- Ernesto 'Che' Guevara, 1965

"Knowledge will forever govern ignorance; and a people who mean to be their own governors, must arm themselves with the power which knowledge gives."

- James Madison, 4th President of the United States of America

6

Table of Contents

Preface

Race. History. Society, and the Media. Even as I mention those words I can picture the rolling eyes and exasperated sighs of friends, family, and acquaintances, mostly -but not always- of a much lighter complexion than my own, who question "why?" Why bring these issues up again? Why can't we simply let bygones be bygones, and move on? I can recall the numerous times in which I've heard the statement made that "I don't see color. I see people", which, if you think about it, isn't even a physical reality. Sometimes, even I question my involvement in such an endeavor; an attempt to understand the link between those four terms - race, history, society, and the media. And when I do, I am reminded not only of my past, and of the legacy and heritage of my people in this country, but also of my daily work in higher education, and of the current realities that the majority of African-Americans -and most middle and lower-class Americans- find themselves facing in the educational, social, judicial, political, and economic realms. I am reminded of the grossly unbalanced inequities that my community, the African-American community, faces everyday in this vast wilderness; in the suburbs and in the inner-cities of this modern-day Superpower known as the United States of America. I think of the struggles, both self-imposed and uncontrollable, that we as a people face. And immediately, my resolve is fortified, and I continue in my endeavor. I ask these questions and engage these topics because they matter, because to ignore or to trivialize them would be to ignore and trivialize the realities that many segments of American society find themselves entrenched in.

And while, like most critics, I am quick to point out the flaws of this country, I am simultaneously grateful to have been born in such an inspiring and pioneering land of opportunity. America, a bastion of *freedom* and, at least until recently, capitalistic superiority; some would say the worlds leading democratic example. I am so grateful, because I know that had I shared the unfortunate reality of being birthed in virtually any other land on this beautiful blue planet of ours, I would have been subject to both the blatantly aggressive as well as the subtly veiled imperialistic aspirations of this great country; especially as a brown-skinned man. Africans know this. Middle Eastern peoples know this. Central and South Americans know this. Mexican, Spanish and Latino peoples know this. Native Americans live with this. Such is the duality of existence for any brown-skinned peoples who are fortunate enough to populate the North American continent; a realization that although this country has a myriad of shortcomings, it will never again (*hopefully*) do to itself what it has done, and is willing to do to both its allies and its enemies, all in the name of democracy. That said, let me state here and now that I am exceedingly *relieved* to be an American! Call it Manifest Destiny, if you will. But know that the majority of the world's citizens call it by another name: imperialism. In the grand scheme of things though, I am without a doubt pro-America. I just so happen to also be pro-freedom, pro-equality, and pro-justice, and sometimes those things don't always go hand-in-hand.

And so it is that I find myself at this keyboard, sitting in front of my computer, about to embark on a journey of understanding. A journey in which the reader and I will attempt to come to grips with the circumstances that this country -and more specifically this country's African-American community- finds itself in. The proceeding pages are not merely an effort to rehash the past, but better yet an exercise in understanding the 'how' and the 'why' of the way that history has played out. Together, the reader and I will delve into the sequence of events that has brought us to our current reality; a country facing economic uncertainty, dealing with both masked and outright social-unease (even under the guise of its first African-American President), a society promoting intellectual death, and a community at a crisis-point – and try to come to some sort of resolution, or understanding, of a means to improve upon these things.

Let me now offer a disclaimer. The reader should immediately close these pages, place this book at their feet, and walk away if he or she is at all closed to the possibility that things may not be as they seem. If the reader is at all apprehensive of the truth, or at least with an earnest and critiquing search for it, then the reader should cut ties now. By no means do I, as the author, make the claim that this text will serve as the definitive source for America's historical perspective. For one, I am nowhere near that knowledgeable nor do I claim to be. Secondly, as everyone knows, history is dictated by the victor, just as beauty is in the eye of the beholder. And as this is my personal search for answers to questions that have plagued me throughout my existence as an African-American male in this country, the discoveries, hypotheses, and conclusions found within this text will be tainted, to a degree, with my insights and beliefs. But to the reader I make a promise to be as balanced and forthcoming as possible. I do not ask that the reader share my beliefs at the conclusion of this work. I only ask that the reader hear mine out, and come to his or her own understanding. Allow me to play the Morpheus to your Neo, if you will…

Shall it be the red pill or the green?

11

Introduction

Along the long and winding road which has been the course of my own educational journey, I have increasingly become intrigued with the study of history; or more to the point, the study of the people and actions that have helped shape our society and the world. I like history because the more familiar one makes him or herself with the situations and circumstances of the past, the more likely that individual is to be able to understand, or to at least begin to grasp the situations and circumstances of the present. I also enjoy the study of history because the closer one honestly and objectively dissects and magnifies the facts of the past the sooner one comes to the realization that history is exactly that: *his*-story. It's the winner's version of the way things went; a running diary of the dominant majority. And if you make the effort to look deeply at what is being said, eventually you will uncover what is actually meant –the implied versus the stated. Like the saying goes, there are at least three sides to every argument: your side, the oppositions' side, and the truth. This book is an attempt to find the balance between the three.

Going forward, there are a few key terms and concepts that the reader will need as a basic backdrop of understanding as we move forward in our conversation. These terms are more than likely ones that you are already familiar with, and the following concepts probably fall into that category as well. However, I'm not too sure that the average reader would make the associations and connections that I intend to.

This information will serve to create a common touch point as we cover the timeline from slavery, the Jim Crow post slavery era, the tumultuous and inspiring Civil Rights Era, the hazy self-indulged and self-medicated 70's, the CIA driven drug explosion and moral decaying of the 80's, the violence and sensational media coverage of the 90's, and the current vacuous-confusion of today's generation. If we are to truly begin the process of understanding each other, it would be helpful that, if for at least once, we began on equal footing.

The Art of War

If you think back to any military movie you may have seen recently or in the past, or even any film whose plot deals with the threat of an extraterrestrial invasion, you'll be hard pressed to find a strategy that does not follow the pattern of first attacking the communication ability of the enemy, followed by the attempt to neutralize the enemy's leadership, which then leads to the demoralization, or complete annihilation of the enemy through sustained attack. Militarily it makes complete sense to follow such a plan of action because once you have disrupted the enemy's ability to communicate you will have successfully created confusion amongst its ranks. If no one can talk to each other then no one can know what the other is doing, especially if the battleground is widespread. It's a fact that in unity there is strength, and if you're unable to even speak with your neighbor then the likelihood of the two of you joining forces is very slim.

And now the next step makes obvious sense. Once you have achieved confusion amongst the ranks of the enemy, then you need only attack from the top-down to create total and utter chaos. Hence, the concept of *killing the messenger* is born. Because once leadership is lost, it will truly be a situation of the blind leading the blind as subordinates will scramble in search of direction from less qualified and battle tested individuals. Once this is accomplished, the task of dividing and conquering the enemy is achieved all the more easily.

There's a reason you see such a pattern over and over again in film and television, and that is because it has been performed over and over again in the real world. Only, in the real world, when dealing with the ever so malleable, reactionary, and impressionable masses that we as human beings tend to be in times of panic, there is one more very important and powerful step that must be taken – the use of propaganda. The American Heritage Dictionary defines propaganda as *the systematic propagation (or spread) of a doctrine or cause, or of information reflecting the views or interests of those advocating such a doctrine or cause.*

Propaganda works in several ways. The first is to build support for the acting agency (the propagators) amongst its constituency (the masses) in its efforts against a perceived enemy by portraying the enemy in a negative, and usually dangerous or threatening light. That is to say, it creates an "us against them" mentality amongst the masses, which the leadership uses to its advantage to gain support for its campaign against "them", whoever they may be. Take Nazi Germany, and Hitler's use of propaganda against the Jews for example. Through the use of constant, sensationalized, and overwhelmingly fabricated propaganda, Hitler was able to galvanize an entire nation of people against a small contingent of its society. Nazi Germany may be the world's most infamous example of the use of propaganda, and its social consequences.

The second aspect of propaganda is that it can eventually begin to work against the psyche of the perceived enemy as this group may now begin to internalize the images and messages being propagated about it. This is usually achieved through sustained, long-term efforts of propaganda. To think of this situation in different terms, let's look at the process of memory, or recall. Repetition of an idea or concept, fact or figure, or any given subject matter over a sustained period of time, eventually leads to the internalization of that subject matter into the thought process or recall of the individual it is being presented to. Therefore, whenever that subject matter is presented, the individual will immediately begin to associate certain characteristics to that subject, even if it only occurs subconsciously.

The third result of propaganda is the flip side of that coin; it can also act as a catalyst which galvanizes the perceived enemy in its efforts against the propagators. Take our current situation in the Middle East for example, and the growth in support of the Jihadist movement, which did not begin until our shift in media coverage went from a search for terrorists to an all out war on Islam. Our media did everything it could to turn our involvement in the Middle East into a holy war, which was a huge mistake on our part, because eventually it actually became one. And in the Middle East, holy wars don't end until there is no one left to fight them. People are not afraid to die when they truly believe that their situation will only improve after death.

If you don't agree, or aren't willing to believe that our media is capable of such underhandedness and trickery, or if you put such actions beyond our loyal and noble government, then I invite you to review the case studies of virtually any conflict in human history between at least two nations, tribes, or sects. Better yet, study this country's tactics in its conflicts during our very own Civil War, in WWI and WWII, Vietnam, the Korean War, the Cold War, Operation Desert Storm, the War on Drugs, and even the current War on Terror. And once you've finished with that exercise, compare the psychological tactics employed in those examples to the media coverage of virtually any Civil Rights Era movement and you will find eerie, if not identical similarities in the portrayal of the perceived enemies. But I digress. We will cover those points in time when they are reached.

These three warfare tactics, disrupting communication, the use of propaganda, and the silencing of the enemy's leadership, are the basic laws of military conduct. They have been proven and tested time and time again, and they work. They are in fact so effective that they have been used in non-military arenas as well. And indeed I intend to make the argument that these tactics have been and continue to be employed in America's constant, but now more subtle, subversive, stealth, and therefore even more impactful war on the African-American community. And yes, your eyes do not deceive you, I said war!

Every Western civilization which has a history in slave trade, be it the United States, the countries of Central and South America, or the islands of the Caribbean, has had to deal with "The Negro Problem". That was the term given to the situation wherein the dominant groups of those civilizations was compelled to come up with a solution to the question of how they would integrate this new group into their own cultural stock. In his paper entitled, "The Education of African People", Asa Hilliard details an exchange between Theodore Roosevelt and an unidentified Brazilian leader in the year 1914. In their conversation, the Brazilian leader offers this insight to Roosevelt:

"Of course the presence of the Negro is a real problem, and a very serious problem, both in your country, the United States, and in mine, Brazil. Slavery was an intolerable method of solving the problem, and had to be abolished. But the problem itself remained, in the presence of the Negro… Now comes the necessity to devise some method of dealing with it. You of the United States are keeping the blacks as an entirely separate element, and you are not treating them in a way that fosters their self-respect. They will remain a menacing element in your civilization, permanent, and perhaps even after a while, a growing element."

- Hilliard, Asa G.; Martin, Luisa. "The Education of African People; Contemporary Imperatives". *Black Child Journal*.

Now the first step in the process of solving a problem, is defining what exactly the problem is - which brings us to the topic of race.

Racial Construction

Something that always puzzled me was the fact that when you look at ethnicities in America, or better yet when one considers the laundry-list of classifications of ethnicities in America, what you typically find are two colors, and numerous ethnic, nationality-designated descriptions that fall somewhere in-between them. Or better yet, for the English majors amongst us, what one typically sees when identifying or describing ethnicities are two adjectives and a myriad of proper nouns. For example: White, English, French, Italian, German, Russian, Persian, Asian, Middle Eastern, Indian, Mexican, Hispanic, Latino, West Indian, African, Black, etc. Looking at that list I am reminded of a song from my childhood which went along the lines of, "which of these things, doesn't belong…"

Of course, for White, one could say Caucasian, and for Black, one could say African-American. But when you honestly think about it, how many of us use the proper terms on a daily basis? And indeed by no means do I make the claim that I consistently use the proper terms either. Quite honestly, it is more convenient to say black and white. However, I believe that there is a more sinister and subconscious reasoning behind our ease of color association; our 'common sense' grouping of the terms. And that the reason is more complex than the simple fact that "White" and "Black" roll off the tongue a little easier than Caucasian and African-American.

The theory of Racial Construction can be summarized into a belief that dominant groups of a specific country, state, or nation, need to organize and categorize the populous into racial groups; in order to create and maintain social norms within that territory. That is to say, that in this country it is easier to say White and Black because the two terms need each other. They are the 'ying' to each other's 'yang', if you will; complementing opposites. In terms of their assignment to a group of people, they determine who is and who isn't. And since they are the extreme opposites of each other, then any other grouping of people or *race* of people, must fall somewhere between the two. It's how social norms are maintained. It's how hierarchies are formed. It's why you have two colors and a litany of nationality-designated ethnicities. In a sense, "Race" is propaganda. Don't believe me? Let's take a look at the definitions of white and black:

white
Pronunciation:

\'hwīt, 'wīt\

Function:
adjective

Inflected Form(s):

whit·er; whit·est

Etymology:

Middle English, from Old English *hwīt;* akin to Old High German *hwīz* white and probably to Old Church Slavic *světŭ* light, Sanskrit *śveta* white, bright

Date:

before 12th century

1 a: free from color **b:** of the color of new snow or milk; *specifically* : of the color white **c:** light or pallid in color <*white* hair> <lips *white* with fear> **d:** lustrous pale gray : SILVERY; *also* : made of silver2 a: being a member of a group or race characterized by light pigmentation of the skin **b:** of, relating to, characteristic of, or consisting of white people or their culture **c**[from the former stereotypical association of good character with northern European descent] **: marked by upright fairness <that's mighty *white* of you>**3: free from spot or blemish: as **a** (1)**: free from moral impurity** : INNOCENT **(2): marked by the wearing of white by the woman as a symbol of purity** <a *white* wedding> **b:** unmarked by writing or printing **c: not intended to cause harm** <a *white* lie> <*white* magic> d: FAVORABLE, FORTUNATE <one of the *white* days of his life — Sir Walter Scott> 4 a: wearing or habited in white **b:** marked by the presence of snow : SNOWY <a *white* Christmas>5 a: heated to the point of whiteness **b:** notably ardent : PASSIONATE <*white* fury>6 a: **conservative or reactionary in political outlook and action** b: **instigated or carried out by reactionary forces as a counterrevolutionary**

measure <a *white* terror>**7:** of, relating to, or **constituting a musical tone quality characterized by a controlled pure sound, a lack of warmth and color, and a lack of resonance8:** consisting of a wide range of frequencies —used of light, sound, and electromagnetic radiation

black

Pronunciation:

\'blak\

Function:

adjective

Etymology:

Middle English *blak,* from Old English *blæc;* akin to Old High German *blah* black, and probably to Latin *flagrare* to burn, Greek *phlegein*

Date:

before 12th century

1 **a:** of the color black **b** (1)**:** very dark in color <his face was *black* with rage> (2)**:** having a very deep or low register <a bass with a *black* voice> (3)**:** <u>HEAVY</u>, <u>SERIOUS</u> <the play was a *black* intrigue>2 **a:** having dark skin, hair, and eyes **:** <u>SWARTHY</u> <the *black* Irish> **b** (1)*often capitalized* **: of or relating to any of various population groups having dark pigmentation of the**

skin <*black* Americans> (2)**: of or relating to the African-American people or their culture** <*black* literature> <a *black* college> <*black* pride> <*black* studies> (3)**:** typical or representative of the most readily perceived characteristics of black culture <trying to sound *black*> <tried to play *blacker* jazz>3**:** dressed in black4**:** <u>DIRTY</u>, <u>SOILED</u> <hands *black* with grime>5 a**:** characterized by the absence of light <a *black* night> **b:** reflecting or transmitting little or no light <*black* water> **c:** served without milk or cream <*black* coffee>6 a**: thoroughly sinister or evil :** <u>WICKED</u> <a *black* deed> **b: indicative of condemnation or discredit** <got a *black* mark for being late>7**: connected with or invoking the supernatural and especially the devil <*black* magic>8 a: very sad, gloomy, or calamitous <*black* despair> b: marked by the occurrence of disaster <*black* Friday>9: characterized by hostility or angry discontent :** <u>SULLEN</u> <*black* resentment filled his heart>10*chiefly British* **:** subject to boycott by trade-union members as employing or favoring nonunion workers or as operating under conditions considered unfair by the trade union11 a*of propaganda* **: conducted so as to appear to originate within an enemy country and designed to weaken enemy morale b:** characterized by or connected with the use of black propaganda <*black* radio>12**:** characterized by grim, distorted, or grotesque satire <*black* humor>13**: of or relating to covert intelligence operations** <*black* government programs>

Cited from Merriam-Webster's Online Dictionary, May 8, 2008

What about those passages stands out to you? Could it be phrases such as "marked by upright fairness", or "free from moral impurity: innocent", or is it "not intended to cause harm: favorable, fortunate" for the explanation of the color white? Could it be such terms as "heavy, serious, swarthy, dirty, soiled, wicked", associated with the color black? Or maybe it's the use of such phrases as "thoroughly sinister or evil...indicative of condemnation or discredit... connected with or invoking the supernatural and especially the devil... marked by the occurrence of disaster... characterized by hostility or angry discontent: sullen", to describe what black is? And consider for a moment the impact of these words and their associations on the impressionable mind of the child learning them for the first time. Consider the impact on the White child and the Black child on day one of their respective journeys into understanding and forming their own identities.

I don't know, maybe I'm just overly sensitive to things like this. Or maybe, just maybe, there's more to this propaganda concept than I thought?

In a 2001, KTEH-PBS discussion concerning racial construction, sociologist- historian, and brilliant thinker Barbara J. Fields, a Professor of American History at Columbia University, argued that "race" is most obviously a product of social processes. And in respect to the racial construction of African-Americans and Caucasians in this country, she explains that, "Freedom did not become possible for Americans of European descent until they had established slavery for Americans of African descent; had defined Afro-Americans as a race and had identified their innate inferiority as a justification, or at least a rationale, for enslavement."

Dr. Fields continues in her train of thought along the lines that it was during the time period of the American Revolution, when the country's 'founding fathers' were in the process of defining what it was to be an American, and therefore defining all of the natural and inherent rights that come along with such a title, that they were at the same time forced to explain the situation of slavery against the juxtaposition of a constitutional claim of 'self evident truths that all men are created equal.' And that through that explanation of the existence of slavery in such an egalitarian environment, the concept of race was born. To quote Dr. Fields, "Bondage does not need justifying as long as it seems to be the natural order of things. You need a radical affirmation of bondage only where you have a radical affirmation of freedom…People holding liberty to be unalienable at the same time that they were holding Afro-Americans as slaves, were bound to end up holding race to be a self-evident truth." So you see, one needed the other. Freedom needed bondage and subservience to define it. White needed Black!

And to me it has always been interesting that it is around this time period in history that you begin to see 'scientific' studies which attempt to 'prove' the differences between the races. I can honestly remember reading in my school history books that it had been 'scientifically' proven that the African slaves had biological deficiencies such as excessive sweat glands, foul odor, and laziness, that the women were overly sexual, and the men nothing more than unintelligible brutes, etc. And I also remember rebuking those claims, even if only in my own young mind, because I knew there were motives behind such findings. One of the biggest problems in today's school system is that the children are still reading those same books. And there is little in the current school system that challenges this view of the peoples we called slaves. There is far too little information available to our students which offers the true nature of the Africans brought to this country; a group of people versed in many languages, from a continent where most of the world's heralded intellectuals of antiquity received their training, and where the world's oldest books and schools are found!

Most sociologists agree with the idea that race is a social construct, based on unfounded and biased-driven pseudo-science, yet race as a concept has still persisted in our common dialogue and scientific jargon. And there are some sociologists that contend that the paramount difference between 'race' and 'ethnicity' is a shared cultural commonality; a common understanding or experience, or more to the point, a bond that goes beyond physical traits and attributes. That said, it is fundamentally important to understand that the African-American experience in this country has, from day one, been designed to prevent any commonality amongst its people – to destroy any bond or sense of community. And so it is all the more clear, to me at least, that racial construction, and even the concept of race itself, is propaganda.

Mechanisms of Subordination

Two more terms for the reader:

Systematic

Sys`tem*at"ic
1. **Of or pertaining to system; consisting in system; methodical; formed with regular connection and adaptation or subordination of parts to each other, and to the design of the whole**; as, a systematic arrangement of plants or animals; a systematic course of study.

2. Proceeding according to system, or regular method; as, a systematic writer; systematic benevolence.
3. Pertaining to the system of the world; cosmical.
These ends may be called cosmical, or systematical. --Boyle.
4. (Med.) **Affecting successively the different parts of the system** or set of nervous fibres; as, systematic degeneration.
Webster's Revised Unabridged Dictionary -

Op·pres·sion

Function: *noun*
: an unjust or excessive exercise of power: as **a** : unlawful, wrongful, or corrupt exercise of authority by a public official acting under color of authority that causes a person harm **b** : dishonest, unfair, wrongful, or burdensome conduct by corporate directors or majority shareholders that entitles minority shareholders to compel involuntary dissolution of the corporation **c** **: inequality of bargaining power resulting in one party's lack of ability to negotiate or exercise meaningful choice**
Merriam-Webster's Dictionary of Law -

By no stretch of the imagination do I believe that these are new concepts for the reader. You've probably heard these two terms before, and more than likely you've heard them combined in reference to some sort of "systemic oppression" that a group of peoples are subject to. It is a social phenomenon that has been present in virtually every society since the beginning societies. It is a reference to the manner in which the dominant group of a particular society ensures that it maintains its dominance; its mechanism of superiority, if you will. However, I feel as though it's a concept that has become so *common sense* within society, so matter-of-fact, that the majority of us have lost its meaning and therefore do not truly grasp its impact.

As the definition of systematic states, the term refers to "consisting in system; methodical, formed with regular connection and adaptation or subordination of parts to each other." The piece that should truly stand out here is *methodical*, or in other words intentional, planned, precise, and carried out continuously. The term *subordination* also stands out glaringly when I read that sentence. To me, the definition of systematic can be reduced to those two terms alone: methodical subordination. Now it is important to note that "methodical subordination" should not necessarily have an evil or negative connotation attached to it. It's a phrase that can describe many of the most basic systems in nature. In a manner of speaking, biological cells have a form of methodical subordination. It refers to a continuous cycle, or intricate system, which is larger than any one part of itself.

So if there is an issue within a system, then to solve one problem within that system is not to offer a solution to the entire scheme. And so it is when dealing with societal issues. To offer say reparations to a group of people in order to ease their plight from centuries of oppression, for example, will do those people no real or permanent good if they have no control or influence over the system in which they will liquidate those reparations. In essence, for there to be real change within a system, there must be several changes made within the system, on several levels of the system.

As where the definition of systematic can still be somewhat obtuse or abstract for some individuals to really grasp and understand, the explanation of oppression is much more to the point. Oppression is defined as an unjust or excessive exercise of power. Again, it is the intentional action of using one's power, or authority, to maintain a position of dominance over another person, group, or organization – in an unfair or unjust manner. It is willful harm committed against another. And now the last stanza of explanation for oppression truly captures, in my opinion, what is implied by the phrase 'systematic oppression'. As I intend to use it, systematic oppression is the *systematically maintained inequality of bargaining power, resulting in one party's lack of ability to negotiate or exercise meaningful choice within that system.*

Capitalism and Corporatism

It's almost comical how smoothly the concept of systematic oppression transitions us to the topic of capitalism, and more appropriately, corporatism. Capitalism is a system built upon the idea of a free market, governed by the concept of supply and demand. Corporatism is the evil twin of capitalism as it fosters an economic environment in which only a handful of corporations are truly in control of the means of production for an entire society, and can therefore dictate the level of supply –i.e., the surplus or deficit- of a particular good, product, or service; think diamonds, oil, or even utilities like electricity and cable, for example.

Historically, we have Adam Smith and Britain's Industrial Revolution to thank for the idea of a laissez-faire economy; an economic system which operates with minimal government interference. The actual practice of capitalism however, would find its teeth during the 16-18th centuries, when England's cloth industry, in response to the American colonies' system of slavery and trade, would see a significant economic boom. The defining aspect of that time period vs. others before it, would be the excess of production over the amount of consumption, and the monetary windfall it created for those in control of the production; due to their ability to dictate the level of supply and therefore the demand.

To be fair, capitalism has proven itself to be the most effective economic structure the world has ever seen; more effective than Socialism and Fascism, with more longevity than Communism. Surely, capitalism has been effective in the sense of growing wealth. However, it has failed in the aspect of spreading wealth. According to 2006 Census Bureau information, there are nearly 20 million households in America with six-figure incomes. Of those households 86.9% were White, and 5.5%, the lowest percentage of any other ethnic group, were African-American. The average median income of all households was $46,326 dollars. The average income for two income earner households was $67,348 dollars. Again, the lowest median household income for any ethnic group was $30,134 dollars for African-Americans. In comparison, the average household income for Asians was $57,518, $48,977 for White households, and $34,241 for Hispanic households.

The term stratification, when used in reference to geology, refers to the layering of rock, or the strata of rock. In terms of its sociological reference, it explains the ranking or hierarchical nature of societies. As Hughes, Kroehler, and Vander Zanden explain, "Social stratification (is) the term sociologists apply to the ranking or grading of individuals and groups into hierarchical layers; (it) represents structured inequality in the allocation of rewards, privileges, and resources." (Hughes, Michael; Kroehler, Carolyn; Vander Zanden, James. Sociology: The Core. McGraw Hill. 2002)

Now in the academic journal, *A Dictionary of Sociology*, Gordon Marshall describes Social Mobility as "the movement – usually of individuals but sometimes of whole groups – between two different positions within the system of social stratification in any society." Furthermore, "It is conventional to distinguish upward and downward mobility; which is to refer to movement up or down a hierarchy of privilege." (Marshall, Gordon: mobility,

social; *A Dictionary of Sociology*. Oxford University Press. 1998)
African-Americans heaviest burden in this country has come in the
form of stagnant social mobility. African-Americans have had to
stand by and watch as virtually every other group of peoples on
this planet have migrated to America, and within the time-span of a
generation, have achieved a higher social standing than
themselves. Again, I make the point that in America you have two
colors, and a myriad of nationality-designated ethnicities that fall
hierarchically between them. And furthermore, since this system
has persisted for over 400 years, through the inclusion of more and
more ethnicities into America's cultural stock, I make the claim
that the result of this country's stratification cannot simply be a
coincidence; it must be systematic.

Now, I'm not as naïve as to actually believe that there will
ever be a society in which every man, woman, and child, of every
background and ethnicity, will be on equal footing financially,
occupationally, educationally, etc. Quite honestly, there is
something substantial to be found within Darwin's theory of
Natural Selection; for when one looks into the world of the wild, it
is true that only the strong survive. There are individuals within
every walk of life that just do not have what it takes to keep up
with society. And in those cases they usually become victims of
the society in which they live, or the weights which hold it down.
Natural Selection as a theory works, for me at least, when the
selection of the 'inferior' occurs naturally, or is made apparent
through the lack of certain natural instincts. However, it does not
explain a human social system in which there is nothing natural
about the selection of the dominant versus the inferior. And it does
nothing to explain a society which actively, or even unconsciously,
promotes the widening of the gap between those with and those
without in a systematic manner.

And so 'Corporatism', in today's context, is more comparable to *Capitalism on performance enhancers*. Corporatism begets corporatism just as greed begets greed. And the problem with that is that the tactics used to gain more money, more power, and more influence, progressively become more and more ruthless. Eventually anything goes in the pursuit of a dollar. Corporatism is the umbrella under which many of society's ails are bred and perpetuated. Greed is an unstoppable virus which has plagued nearly every social and economic system since the beginning of societies. Today, conglomerations have found it far too profitable to play upon the insecurities, fears, desires, and flat out ignorance of society, to ever take a step back and consider whether or not they should. Our very own economic system has become an all-out attack on our physical, mental, and spiritual sensibilities!

One such consequence of the play on society's insecurities is serious health problems, namely eating disorders, which occur among many young and middle-aged American women of all ethnicities, as they push themselves to reach unattainable and unnatural physical standards set forth by mainstream media and popular culture. According to a report produced by the National Eating Disorder Association, "In the United States, as many as 10 million females and 1 million males are fighting a life and death battle with an eating disorder such as anorexia or bulimia. Millions more are struggling with binge eating disorder (Crowther et al., 1992; Fairburn et al., 1993; Gordon, 1990; Hoek, 1995; Shisslak et al., 1995)." (www.nationaleatingdisorders.org) This phenomenon is the product of Hollywood's, as well as the fashion industry and the general pop-culture's fascination and glorification of the extremely skinny and waif individual. The individuals deemed most desirable by the talking heads of screen and magazine are quite simply not healthy, yet we find no problem in persuading our youth the emulate them.

Another often recognized but seldom challenged - at least to any avail - reality in the entertainment and fashion industry, is the glorification of Caucasian features as being the most beautiful and most desirable traits of entertainers and models. The "blonde hair, blues eyes" syndrome is yet another example of the subtle and subversive tactics used to maintain institutionalized racism, as well as the cause of widespread depression amongst brown-skinned men and women who do not fit this ideal. To this day it is a constant theme on the "Top 10, 50, or 100" lists and countdowns of VH1 and the E! Channel, or Maxim, FHM, and Vogue magazines, or in the casting offices of Hollywood executives.

The idolization of Caucasian features, and the glorification of the unnatural physique is an attack on our physical well-being. And in some ways, it's even a play on our mental capacities as well. But this country's true impact on society's intellect comes in the form of educational funding and reform; or more to the point, the lack thereof.

Any economist will tell you that a country's economic system will experience cyclical highs and lows throughout its timeline. And currently, America is a facing a slumping economy, or more to the point an all-out economic crisis, which in several parts of the country is due in large part to companies outsourcing for cheaper labor, a nation-wide unstable home loan and mortgage system, and a general decline in education amongst our workforce. Also, the reality of our dependence on things like automobiles, technology, and oil which are predominantly provided by outside nations, does nothing to help our country's bottom line. The value of the U.S. dollar against the Euro has fallen dramatically. And in the ever questionable decision-making of the Bush Administration someone came up with the quick-fix idea of a "stimulus check" for American taxpayers - a check that more than likely went towards the purchase of more outsourced goods. It has never been more apparent than now that for the last eight years, this nation has been led by a marginal student. Yet ironically, any discussion of educational reform in this country is quickly tabled for *more pressing* issues. But I ask you dear reader, what can be more pressing than the education of tomorrow's leaders; the education of today's youth?

It was the 1954 Supreme Court decision in Brown v. Board of Education that overruled the "separate but equal" doctrine of Plessy v. Ferguson (1896), and un-segregated American schools. Of course, the decision was met with strong resistance, and it would be many years, as well as take the deployment of thousands of National Guard troops, before many of America's educational institutions would adhere to the ruling. And once it became clear that integration wasn't going anywhere any time soon, those individuals with the means to do so banded together to create a surge in the enrollment of private schools; the new and completely legal form of segregation. From that point on, around the mid 1970's, American public and private schooling have been on two separate paths – one, on a constant upward trend in funding and quality, the other, in a state of crises, as the states themselves have found other more pressing issues to funnel their funds towards. And what the American educational system has been left with is an education achievement gap.

And our economy is beginning to feel it. The less educated individuals that a society has entering its workforce, the more it has to rely on other sources of labor; the more it has to outsource for resources that it used to produce in abundance. As we speak, America is producing less and less of its own natural resources, and becoming more and more dependant upon outside sources: enter an Indian workforce, Chinese production, Arabian Oil, and Japanese technology. Don't worry though, if we've learned anything from our current situation, in the years to come our educational funding will more than likely continue to shrink, but our "stimulus checks" should continue to grow. As Gary Phillups, chief scientist for the American Institutes for Research in Washington, D.C. explains, "In a global economy, the best jobs are not going to the best in your class but to the best in the world." (Kenneth Terrell,*"Virginia School Tops America's Best High Schools List"*; U.S. News and World Report. December 5, 2008)

    The final blow to the morality and psyche of our overly capitalistic society has come in the provocative, sensual, and seductive form of **sex**. As they say, 'sex sells', and it seems as if everyone in the world of media has bought into this approach hook-line-and sinker. The very next time you have the opportunity, just take a quick glance at some of the sexual undertones and provocative attire found in most Disney programs which cater to the preteen audience. As author Juliet B. Schor states in her book Born to Buy, "The Janet Jackson (Superbowl) and Nicolette Sheridan (Monday Night Football) incidents hit a nerve because they tapped into the fact that parents are worried about another trend: the premature sexualization of their daughters through their participation in the consumer culture. Unlike television, which at least has a ratings system, a V-Chip, and an off button, the rest of consumer culture isn't as easy to tune out." (Juliet B. Schor. Born to Buy; Scribner. 2004, p.215)

    And this is where, in my opinion at least, the average American family has taken its hardest hit. The fallout of such over-sexualized media content, whether it be in magazines, on television, in the movies, or in music, has been the decimation of the American Nuclear family. And in recent years, a sharp increase of promiscuity and sexually-transmitted diseases amongst young and middle-aged adults in American communities underscores that sentiment. I personally believe the average young to middle aged American has become a victim of the constant sexual stimulation offered by the media, and the result is that many Americans find it difficult to stay satisfied, and sometimes faithful, in a long-term relationship -especially when everything they see and hear encourages them to enjoy the passion of the moment with any willing stranger. There's a reason that the ABC series Desperate Housewives was so well received amongst the American public.

And what about our young women? What affect does this have on them? As a result of our sex-heavy media content, be it in movies, magazines, or music videos, our young women have become more and more willing to utilize their sexuality, ahead of any other skill-set, to get ahead in life; or to accumulate material wealth. I offer the "Video Ho" phenomenon as exhibit 'A'. These young women constantly receive the message that sex can get them paid; it can get them cars, clothes, or homes. It can propel them to fame - even though what we now call fame we used to categorize as infamy – and so they flock to any and every video set from L.A. to Miami hoping to be chosen, waiting for the opportunity to shake it for the cameras.

Over-sexualized media content is the real 'threat to the American institution of marriage', as President George W. Bush refers to same-sex marriage. In the big scheme of things, same-sex marriage doesn't even rank. But for good old G. W., and the rest of our government, it has been a hell of a distraction!

Capitalism thrives on certain unspoken, unwritten tenets, but none are more profitable or institutionalized than the American Dream itself. The powers that be have always sold the ideal of the American Dream as the promise of freedom and the opportunity to improve ones social standing. The unattainable carrot of advancement which dangles from the stick of debt. But the American governments own interpretation of the American Dream is itself capitalism and exploitation of the masses; both domestically and globally. Domestically, at least for Americans on the lower end of the socioeconomic totem-pole, this plays itself out in the form of limited social mobility; the proverbial glass ceiling. Globally, the rest of the worlds nations have come to realize the true intentions of America's democratic front, and they have begun to defend themselves against our imperialistic tendencies, and use our government's greed and lack of foresight against it. Hence, oil prices continue to rise, the Euro strengthens as the dollar weakens, and China and Japan deal with the U.S. on their own terms, if at all.

And it is our government, which many of the nations companies and conglomerations have their well-oiled and well-funded tentacles entrenched in, that either stands idly by or in some instances actively hides the realities of our nations capitalistic aspirations - and their affect on our communities, from the individuals they effect most immediately; the American people. Currently, our country's problems go much deeper, and cover far more ground than simply Black and White matters. These days, there isn't much media coverage regarding public outcry about outright racial issues, so much as there is a general concern over systematically maintained institutions of disadvantage (i.e., primary and secondary education, higher education, the penal system, etc.)

There has been a shift of "isms", if you will. And that shift has moved up the color spectrum from black to green; from outright Racism to all-out Corporatism. It has created a situation where even members of the dominant majority have come to feel so isolated from the privileges of their ethnic peers, that they have begun to associate with, identify with, and emulate their brothers and sisters - their comrades in the struggle for self-respect and human recognition. Or more to the point, they have begun to resemble, if only in style and plight, their African-American brethren.

I give you the very talented and gifted entertainer Eminem for example, a young White male so adept at rhyming that he has the ability to put most of his African-American peers to shame with his lyricism and deft delivery- but make no mistake about it, he learned to do so by emulating African-Americans. Was it his fascination of the African-American culture, the harsh realities of growing up in Detroit's mean streets, or the flat out hunger to succeed and improve he and his daughters societal and financial standing that drove young Marshal Matthers to greatness? No one will ever truly know but him. However I would venture to say that it was a combination of all three.

African-Americans have always been trend-setters. Since the beginning of American society, or at least the pop-culture aspect of it, African-Americans have set the tone for what is cool, what is hip, and what the youth want to emulate. As Washington Post writer Donna Britt offers, "No wonder so many black men seek to develop the wardrobe, attitude and facial expressions that telegraph cool. No other group's identity is as steeped in the necessity of appearing cool, or in the expectation that they instinctively bring coolness to the table." (Staff. <u>Being a Black Man</u>. Washington Post: 2007) We have always been innovators on the forefront of trends, even if we never received credit for the trends themselves!

With respect to the power of African-American trend-setting influence, I am reminded of an incident I witnessed while I was in college. I was returning to the Pacific Northwest after a trip home to visit friends and family. As I waited curbside for a friend to pick me up outside of Seattle-Tacoma International airport, I remember overhearing two older White gentlemen in conversation. One of the men had to be in his mid to late 50's, while the other may have been closer to his late forties or early 50's. Anyhow, they were discussing some high-end business which no doubt involved profit-margins and stock options, when along came a Black SUV with tinted windows and what had to be at least 22" rims. The driver was a young petite White woman. I couldn't help but chuckle to myself as the two men entered the vehicle, because I knew exactly where the customization concept of that vehicle, for this particular group at least, had come from – Black America and Hip-Hop.

In mainstream America's attempt to demonize and vilify everything African-American, it has quite often had the reverse affect amongst mainstream youth, effectively elevating the African-American community, or at least many aspects of its community – some positive, most negative - to a level of envy and fascination within the young and impressionable minds of mainstream youth. And at first, America didn't know how to react.

When Elvis stole and emulated the music and dance moves of young African-Americans, with his soulful crooning and gyrating hips, mainstream America tried to ban him from TV screens and radio stations. In its infancy, Jazz was seen as the devil's music; a bastardization of the gospel. And in the 1990's Gangster Rap was seen as so anti-authority, so anti-American, that American politicians ardently tried to have it banned, but only succeeded in having it censored – *slightly*. In reality, conservative America's immediate reaction to all of these subjects, only served to boost mainstream America's, and the rest of society's interest in said subjects; it created the phenomenon of the "forbidden fruit" that must be tasted. And after its initial shock, it wasn't long before the powers that be in mainstream America, namely those in control of the media, realized there was far too much money to be made in the exploitation of these individuals and genres, to ever have them banned. On the contrary, once the power brokers behind American media realized the earning potential behind these issues, they did all they could to bring them to every television set, radio station, and magazine, in search of access to the wanting public; including those who wanted nothing to do with them at all.

A final concept...

Media Studies

Media literacy is the process of accessing, analyzing, evaluating and creating messages in a wide variety of forms. It uses an inquiry-based instructional model that encourages people to ask questions about what they watch, see and read. It provides tools to help people critically analyze messages to detect propaganda, censorship, and bias in news and public affairs programming (and the reasons for such), and to understand how structural features -- such as media (*or conglomerate*) ownership, or its funding model -- affect the information presented. Media literacy aims to enable people to be skillful creators and producers of media messages, both to facilitate an understanding as to the strengths and limitations of each medium, as well as to create independent media.

- Definition provided by Wikipedia.com

As was mentioned before, the intent of this book is not merely an attempt to recount the happenings of the past, or simply re-tell history from a different perspective. Rather it is an attempt at understanding how we have come to be in our current state. It is an attempt to understand how we have come to live in a society in which we are all too easily distracted from the serious social issues which plague us; such as our unbalanced and underfunded educational system, the daily realities that many of our youth face, our –up until very recently at least- lack of competent leadership, a media system that promotes ignorance and stupidity amongst the populous, and the over-arching economy that has benefitted, but now slumps because of it all. The intent of this book is to analyze this situation and grasp for the solution to these issues; to look deeply, and honestly at America, and more specifically the African-American community, and to tell them both the truth about themselves in the hopes that once they see their shortcomings for what they really are, they may find the courage to address and fix them.

I believe that Media Studies may offer us the opportunities and the tools to at least begin this process. Through media studies we will be able to arm ourselves and our youth with the weapons we will need – a questioning mind, a respect for but not a fear of authority, courage, and most important of all, knowledge – as we face our mortal enemies; greed, racism, sexism, and several other 'isms', in a struggle for survival and prosperity in this vast wilderness that we call America, and our global community. As I see it, media studies are a spring board from which one will unintentionally -but unavoidably- be catapulted into several separate but linked fields of inquiry; history, sociology, economics, and international relations. This book is an attempt to transform *his* story into *our* story, because I'd like to think that once individuals believe that we all have a stake in this country's future, perhaps we will all begin to work together towards improving it.

Chapter 1

Slavery and Jim Crow

Several years from now, the significance, the importance, and the poignancy of 2008 Presidential candidate Senator Barack Obama's "A More Perfect Union" speech will more than likely be lost upon the masses. The honesty and candor with which Senator Obama addressed the nation on Tuesday, March 18, 2008, has not been seen for some time, and will not likely be seen for some time again.

The speech was a response to the controversial remarks made by Obama's long time friend, mentor, and pastor, Chicago based Reverend Jeremiah Wright. In truth, it was more a response to the media's reaction to the Rev.'s remarks and the Clinton campaigns attempt to link Senator Obama to the ideologies espoused by the religious leader, than a response to the comments themselves. Senator Obama's speech however, was beyond reproach. There was no partisanship to be found in the oratory. No playing to this side or that. No pacifying of lobbyists. No pontificating to liberal or conservative. No, in Senator Obama's speech, no such rhetoric could be found. What was there, in plain sight for all to see, was an intelligent and informed opinion of the true issues which ail this country -and rob it of its true potential- coupled with an explanation of the manner in which we may begin to heal our nation. As the Senator stated:

"The fact is that the comments that have been made and the issues that have surfaced over the last few weeks reflect the complexities of race in this country that we've never really worked through – a part of our union that we have yet to perfect. And if we walk away now, if we simply retreat into our respective corners, we will never be able to come together and solve challenges like healthcare, or education, or the need to find good jobs for every American."

- Senator Barack Obama. "A More Perfect Union"; Delivered Tuesday, March 18, 2008. Philadelphia, PA

What I particularly liked about Obama's approach to this speech was the way in which he infused a history lesson into the framing of, and not excuse for, the reverend's comments. He then took that framing to present a challenge to the audience, and more broadly to America, to use this opportunity to learn from and to grow towards becoming a better, more educated, and more understanding society.

Those are my intentions with this book; this commentary on American society. Together we will explore the historical factors that have brought us to the reality of today. We will infuse today's consciousness with a respect for and awareness of the past. We will be reminded that although the legalized practice of slavery may have ended nearly 140 years ago, the Civil Rights Movement of the 1960's occurred only 40 years ago. And when looking at the Achievement Gap in education, when looking at the distribution of wealth in this country, when looking at crime and poverty rates, incarceration or health statistics, we will not offer an excuse for these circumstances, rather we will begin to frame their truths within the context of the situations that have caused and perpetuated them.

We will understand that there is reasoning behind the fact that the most frequent and emphasized images of Black and Brown people in our media system are violent, ignorant, over-sexualized or otherwise derogatory. And we will not be complacent to continue to stand by and watch as we lose a generation of young minds to these negative and stereotypical images and messages. No! We simply cannot and will not let this happen. We must make a stand here and now! And so, if we are to begin anywhere on our search for understanding, we must start at the beginning. We must start at slavery.

Slavery

"We do not need to recite here the history of racial injustice in this country. But we do need to remind ourselves that so many of the disparities that exist in the African-American community today can be directly traced to inequalities passed on from an earlier generation that suffered under the brutal legacy of slavery and Jim Crow."

- Senator Barack Obama. "A More Perfect Union"; Delivered Tuesday, March 18, 2008. Philadelphia, PA

The purpose of examining slavery here is not simply to rehash the horrors of this American nightmare. It is not to focus on the death and enslavement of over 100 million African peoples. More intently, the purpose of this section is to look at the influence of this time period on the American and African-American communities. And make no mistake about it, at this point in the American timeline, those are certainly two distinct groups.

The American institution of slavery was perhaps the most divisive and destructive system of cultural destruction the world has ever known. And yes, it is true that slavery has existed in human societies even since before history was recorded. It was present in ancient Babylon, Persia, Egypt, Greece, Rome and Asia Minor. Interestingly enough though, even in those ancient times, and in those ancient primitive (or so some would have you believe) civilizations, there were commonly accepted laws which protected slaves from the abuses of their slave masters. Slaves in those ancient societies filled many social roles, from laborers, to sculptors and artisans, and were even instructors in some cases. And the emancipation of slaves from slavery was also a common occurrence in those civilizations, so much so in fact, that emancipated slaves, or 'freedmen', began to seriously affect the social system of Ancient Rome. (*Slavery*. The Columbia Encyclopedia: Sixth Edition. 2008) What distinguishes the American institution of slavery from virtually any other form of slavery before it, was the dedicated dismantling and systematic destruction of the indentured peoples culture and sense of self.

The African continent has proven itself to be home to some of the world's oldest known skeletal structures and artifacts. In fact, in February of 2005, United States and Ethiopian scientists unearthed the remains of the oldest hominid skeletal structure to date. The remains, found in the Afar region of Ethiopia, are estimated to be between 3.8 and 4 million years old, nearly 1 million years older than the remains of Lucy, the name given to the previous hominid record holder discovered in 1974, some 40 miles from the 05' discovery. ("Scientists unearth early skeleton". BBC News: March, 7, 2005)

Indeed, the pyramids of Egypt are dated to have been under construction as far back as 3200 B.C. ("NOVA: This Old Pyramid". Aired August, 1, 2006; www.pbs.org), a date much older than the 1600's in which the first Africans arrived in the British settlements of the East Coast. I make this point to emphasize the fact that for centuries upon centuries, Africa, and more importantly Africans, were thriving and living just fine before any Portuguese or Dutch or English ships invaded their shores. These peoples had languages, cultures, traditions, and histories long before they were kidnapped and bartered for; long before they were brought to this country and *forced* to forget all of that.

"Under penalty of death" was a phrase that every slave understood from day one of their American experience. It was the law of the land that no slaves should congregate, for fear of organization, and if two or more slaves were found congregating they could be punished under penalty of death. Remember the rules of war? The first step is always to cut off communication. And along those lines, any attempt at education or discovery of literacy was punishable under penalty of death. Indeed, any slave caught teaching, or attempting to teach other slaves would fall victim to the most brutal lynching. *Kill the messenger.* When slaves were auctioned off, it was practice to purchase no more than a handful of slaves from any particular tribe or region for fear that they would be able to communicate with each other, and therefore organize against the slave master. This practice falls under the objective of divide and conquer.

It is common knowledge that families were disbanded and spread throughout the land; babies ripped from their mothers' arms, fathers and mothers, husbands and wives, brothers and sisters all separated from one another and sent their separate ways. All of this was done, intentionally, to disorient the African in the New World; to destroy any sense of community amongst the Africans. It was done to prevent unity. There is a reason that African-American households have been stereotypically depicted as matriarchal in structure. And the reasoning stems from the fact that in the time of slavery, families were torn apart, with the father being either sold and relocated or used as a stud, much in the manner that thoroughbred horses are used today. It was the mother who kept and reared the children until they were of suitable age to be put to work or sold. As a community moves forward through time, accustomed to this sort of familial structure, it begins to harden itself to certain realities. African-American women became the ultimate bedrock of black families, as they had to be prepared for the absence of their African-American men. And in some cases, African-American women were the bedrock of the white families that owned them, as they were the ones responsible for the rearing of the children, the preparing of the food, and the maintenance of the home.

But it is only the latter half of this story, what slaves couldn't do or were unable to do, that is emphasized in the studies of American History in today's elementary classrooms. Students are only ever taught the shortcomings of the peoples we called slaves, without ever really grasping the brevity of the circumstances which caused or influenced those shortcomings. Sure, students learn about the magnificence of ancient Egypt, and of the pyramids. They learn of the complexity of the ancient civilizations of Mesopotamia and Samaria. But what of the African peoples on the Western Coast of Africa? What of their culture and history do our students learn? Very little if anything I'd imagine, because to give those peoples an identity, to give them a culture and a sense of tradition, would amplify the atrocities of the slave trade, and the savagery of those who profited from it. In essence, to civilize the West Africans, would be to un-civilize the slave traders and the system of slavery. As African-American intellectual, philosopher, and Professor, Dr. Asa G. Hilliard stated:

"The calculated strategy of suppressing and falsifying our history, suppressing and stigmatizing our identity, and propagandizing us with teaching(s) of white supremacy, is something that continues today in both overt and covert forms. The primary purposes of all these forms of oppression was to divide, and therefore dominate us... This is why the historical culture war on Africans was waged, to prevent any reemergence of ethnic consciousness among us, to prevent the unity that will lead to effective mobilization of our efforts as a group and to effective resistance to opposition."

- Dr. Asa G. Hilliard III, "What Do We Need To Know Now?", 1999

Falsifying and Propagandizing

In a chapter focused on Religion, Education, and Medicine in the 6th edition of the Sociology textbook entitled, *Sociology; The Core* (McGraw Hill, 2002), by Michael Hughes, Carolyn Kroehler, and James Vander Zanden, the authors explain the Conflict and Functionalist theories for the purpose of public schooling as such:

"In large, conflict-ridden, multiethnic societies like the United States, the schools become instruments to Americanize minority people. Compulsory education erodes ethnic differences and loyalties and transmits to minorities and those at the bottom of the social hierarchy, the values and lifeways of the dominant group... Functionalists say that the education system functions to inculcate the dominant values of a society and shape a national mind."

In both theories, the basic idea is that in a society such as America - a diverse and dynamic conglomerate of numerous peoples from numerous ethnic backgrounds with a myriad of cultural upbringings and perspectives - it is in the best interest of the dominant majority to sculpt an educational system that is unifying in the interests of the majority. That said, the task of the dominant group then becomes one in which a common and positive perspective of the country must be sculpted from the events of that country's past. In essence, it's in the best interests of the country's leadership to shape a public school system that introduces and reinforces only the positive aspects of that country. In doing so, certain realities must be softened, changed, or all together omitted from the educational discourse; certain things must be falsified and certain ideas must be propagated. Schools have become pathways to socialization rather than enlightenment.

One of the pivotal moments of my intellectual and developmental life occurred in my freshman year of college. My roommate and I would sometimes wax philosophical about all sorts of topics, and it was on one of these occasions that he offered some eye-opening insight. I'm not quite sure as to the exact nature of our discussion, but I do know that it revolved around our respective frustration with our parents. You know, your standard "they just don't understand where I'm coming from" type of conversation. Anyhow, it was during this talk that my roommate said "You know, your parents are people too. They're really just you with about 20 more years worth of experience. But they've made mistakes too."

It was at that moment that something clicked. I began to look at my parents in a different light. And that is not to say that I began to view them in a negative or unappreciative manner, but I began to realize the true weight of my friend's words. My parents were fallible. They were people too, and they were once my age and had gone through all the trials and tribulations that I had gone through, or were about to undertake. But more than that, I began to deconstruct the pedestal that I had placed my parents on. I began to see them as people, instead of the 'all-knowing' superheroes that I had built them up to be; truly a pivotal moment for any person on the path towards adulthood.

I feel that the same discovery needs to be made with respect to the historical figures of this country; the George Washington's, Abraham Lincoln's, and Thomas Jefferson's of this country – the Founding Fathers, if you will - the people that our history books have built skyscraper tall pedestals under. Americans need to know that the country wasn't the only thing these men were fathering, so to speak. They need to know that George Washington had illegitimate children with his slaves. They need to know that 'Old Honest Abe' really didn't want to free the slaves, and that the civil war was not necessarily fought over slavery; it was more a conflict over economics and a Southern social system. People need to know how Lincoln truly felt:

"I am not nor have (I) ever been in favor of bringing about in any way the social and political equality of the black and white races. That I am not, nor ever have been, in favor of making voters or jurors of negroes, nor qualifying them to hold office, nor to intermarry with white people; and I will say in addition to this that there is a physical difference between the *white and black races* which will ever forbid the two races living together on terms of social and political equality. And inasmuch as they cannot so live, while they do remain together, there must be the position of superior and inferior, and I, as much as any other man, am in favor of having the superior position assigned to the White race."

(4th Lincoln-Douglas debate, 18ix. Collected Works Vol. 3, p.145-146)

Our students need to know that Lincoln actually supported segregation and slavery. And they need to understand this so that they can begin to deconstruct the mental pedestal that the American school system has placed Abraham Lincoln and so many others of his time upon. They need to know this so that they can begin to see Lincoln as he really was; a product of his time, instead of the altruistic idol we have made him out to be. Our youth are often times smarter than we think, or at least, able to understand more than we would probably prefer. So along those lines, we need to begin treating them, not as adults, but as thinking, rationalizing individuals. Believe me, they can take it. If they can take everything else that society and the media throws at them, they can also take the truth about the past.

The Emancipation Proclamation, for example, didn't free all of the slaves; its true focus was on the states in secession from the union. The southern border-states which had stayed loyal to the Union - Delaware, Maryland, Kentucky, and Missouri - continued in their practice of slavery well past Lincoln's empty proclamation. ("Civil War". The Columbia Encylopedia; 6th Edition. Cited 2008) As a matter of fact, the Emancipation Proclamation actually stated that if the states in rebellion returned to the Union within 100 days they would be allowed to maintain the institution of slavery.

Whatever the true impetus behind the Civil War (1861-1865), the conflict did serve to leave the nation with its first form of centralized government. However, in terms of real and impactful reform with regards to race-relations in this country, it did little else. Sure, slavery, or at least the federally recognized form of it may have ended shortly after the fighting, but as soon as slaves had tasted their *freedom*, other mechanisms of oppression were put into place, such as the Black Codes and Jim Crow Laws, which sustained their station in daily life. These regulations and restrictions on civil liberties effectively maintained the institution of slavery and the position of subservience in the Black community. Opposition to the inclusion of the African peoples as equals in American society was so strong in fact, that it would cost the embattled Abraham Lincoln his life, as a group of Southern loyalists led by John Wilkes Booth, planned and successfully carried out the assassination of the President, and very nearly assassinated his Vice President Andrew Johnson, Secretary of State William Seward, and Secretary of War Edwin Stanton.

That same year, however, Congress would establish an organization titled the Bureau of Refugees, Freedmen, and Abandoned Lands; which would come to be known as the Freedman's Bureau. (McElrath, Jessica. "The Freedman's Bureau": About.com; 2007, cited 6/5/08) The Bureau would have to survive several veto attempts by President Elect Johnson. And although it only sustained for 6 years (it was originally proposed for 1), the Freedman's Bureau would have the most positive impact on the African-American community of any government organization or legislature for the next 100 years. The Bureau would go on to build over 1,000 schools, which include several of today's Historically Black Colleges. The Bureau also granted nearly 850,000 acres worth of land to freed slaves, but was thwarted once again by President Johnson, who bequeathed the land right back to Confederate land owners.

The very next year, 1866, would be a year which saw the Civil Rights Bill passed even after the unsuccessful veto attempt of Johnson. In doctrine only, this piece of legislature would give full citizenship rights to Blacks. And almost in direct response to the government's attempt to equal the playing field for African-Americans, no matter how transparent or half-hearted the attempts themselves may have been, an extreme faction of Confederate Army veterans would form an organization known as the Ku Klux Klan, better known as the KKK, in Pulaski, Tennessee.

Domestic Terrorism

It is important to recognize that there are really several distinct phases in the lifespan of the hate based organization known as the Ku Klux Klan. In the initial phase the group began as a social club for former Confederate militants, and quickly evolved into a terrorist organization. As Richard Wormser reports in his piece on the KKK for the PBS documentary entitled "The Rise and Fall of Jim Crow", "From 1869 to 1871 (the Klan's) goal was to destroy reconstruction by murdering blacks – and some whites – active either in Republican politics or educating black children". Basically, they resisted, by deadly force, any activities of the Freedman's Bureau. They referred to themselves as the Invisible Empire of the South, and they intimidated the freed Black population by burning their homes, churches, schools, and sometimes even the people themselves. Lynching became a common threat tactic employed by the Klan, and both Blacks and their white Bureau supporters were their targets. It wasn't until Congress passed the Force Bill in 1871, which gave the government the power to prosecute Klan members and the Klan itself for its actions, that the outright offenses against Blacks and Bureau members, in the name of the Klan at least, began to subside. (Richard Wormser. Ku Klux Klan: The Rise and Fall of Jim Crow. PBS. 2002) Once Congress started inquiring about the actions of the Klan, the organization began to loose favor amongst conservative southerners and their political leaders. Or at least that is what the popular opinion of the time would have one believe.

This would mark the end of the first phase of the Klan, and usher in a time period of 'cloaked' Klan activity; cloaked under the pretense of public outcry. As Eliza Steelwater states in her book entitled The Hangman's Knot, "Lynchings came to be presented differently – a theatrical spectacle that said, 'The community has come together in a spontaneous outpouring of outrage against an African-American who committed an atrocity'." (Eliza Steelwater. The Hangman's Knot: Westview Press. 2003) So now, when the Klan, or other willing community members felt the need to make an example of, or punish an African-American, they no longer had to hide under the shadow of nightfall, or under the cover of bed sheets, they could simply rouse enough support from within the community to corner and torture the offender to death in plain sight for all to see. In fact, many of those lynched were handed over to the mobs by the very policemen whose job it was to protect them.

It was during this time period in particular, the Reconstruction era of the South, that things got really bad for African-Americans in this country; especially for African-American males. Southern society was based upon the existence of a subservient, lower-class which consisted primarily of slaves. Once the slaves had been set-free, the White southern majority felt the need to maintain their dominant position by any means necessary; through fear, intimidation, degradation, and more often than not, death.

There are several sources to find statistics which guess at the number of lynchings during this time period, particularly the years between 1882 and the mid 1950's, but none are completely accurate. One reason for their inaccuracy is that the statistics are based primarily upon lynching reported by the newspapers of the time. And as was hinted at previously, most lynching which took place during the first phase of the KKK was preformed in secrecy rather than in public view. Also, the geography of the South is predominantly rural; therefore there are certainly murders which went under the radar of the press. Another factor which might undermine the integrity of the stats is the lack of an agreed upon definition of what constitutes a lynching. Of the definitions I came across, I prefer the explanation given by Robert Gibson in his work entitled, The Negro Holocaust, in which he describes lynching as "open public murders of individuals suspected of crime, conceived and carried out more or less spontaneously by a mob." Regardless, the figures range from the mid-4,000's to over 5,000, conservatively. And those numbers also take into account the lynching of White Americans, although they are a decided minority in the figures (at about a 4:1 or 5:1 ratio, if not more).

As was mentioned before, this was an especially dangerous time period for African-American males. Make no mistake about it however, African-American women and White men and women found associating with African-Americans, as well as any other minority in the country during that time period were potential victims of lynching. The large disparity in the numbers for African-American males lay in the fact that the majority of the accusations which lead to lynching were those of murder or rape; and rape was as broadly defined as looking at a white woman. It also didn't require any further investigation; if a White woman said a Black man raped her, any available Black man was guilty. Angry mobs don't rely on judges or juries to convict the accused, they do it themselves, and once a black man was accused of any wrongdoing, the mob convicted him. Southern politicians actually referred to such practices as "lynch law". Accusations which would make one eligible for lynch law consideration ranged from the more serious grievances previously mentioned, to more trivial offences such as "disputing with a white man, attempting to vote, unpopularity, self-defense, or general 'insult to white persons'."

(Robert Gibson. The Negro Holocaust: Yale-New Haven Teachers Institute. 2008) The occurrence of lynching would not cease for some time. But in 1922, in response to the passing of Senator Leonidas Dyer of Missouri's Anti-Lynching Bill in the House of Representatives, the fear of government mandated punishment for lynching participation would cause a significant decrease in the annual number of incidents; or at least in the reported number of incidents.

On a quick side note - for those of you who think of the Ku Klux Klan as a relic or figment of the past – the following passage comes directly from the official website of The Knights Party, "The Knights Party is the 6th era of the Ku Klux Klan…Our goal is to win political power. All the things we hope to achieve can be wrapped up in winning political power…We are reaching out to people on the premise of their need for political alternatives. We recognize that Christianity and political activism cannot be separated." (Rachel Pendergraft. What is 33/6; Source: The Official Website of The Knights Party, USA. 2008) Just something to think about…

....

The Big Picture

1) 1st Wave of American Immigration (1640-1820) – German settlers and other Europeans; especially in Pennsylvania
- **Naturalization Act of 1790**; stayed on record until 1952

- "Be it enacted by the Senate and House of Representatives of the United States of America in Congress assembled, That any alien, being a free white person, who shall have resided within the limits and under the jurisdiction of the United States for the term of two years, may be admitted to become a citizen thereof, on application to any common law court of record, in any one of the states wherein he shall have resided for the term of one year at least, and making proof to the satisfaction of the court, that he is a person of good character, and taking an oath of affirmation prescribed by law, to support the constitution of the United States, which oath or affirmation such court shall administer; and the clerk of such court should record such application, and the proceedings thereon; and thereupon such person shall be considered as a citizen of the United States."

(Statutes at Large, First Congress; Session II, Chapter 3, p. 103-104. 1790)

   - Act naturalized "free white" immigrants, and their children; born domestically and abroad. It left out however, all indentured servants, slaves, free African-Americans, and later on Asian immigrants.
2) 2nd Wave of American Immigration (1820-1880) – German and Irish, as well as Chinese laborers
- Industrial Revolution

3) 3rd Wave of American Immigration (1880-1924) – Italians, Eastern Europeans, as well as Japanese and Filipino immigrants
- **Chinese Exclusion Act of 1882**
- **Gentleman's Agreement of 1908**
- The timeframe of the Great Migration as well
- New immigrants bring spark in different industries; garments, movies, agriculture, fishing, and franchise banking
- World War I: 1914-1918

4) **Immigration Act of 1924**; remained in place until 1965

....

Chapter 2:

The African-American response and the shift in America's Demographics

Between the time period of the 1870's until about 1915, over 25 million European immigrants came in mass from Italy, Germany, Russia, Portugal, Ireland, Poland, Slovakia, etc., in search of better life opportunities, freedom of religion, and every other type of opportunity that people migrate to new lands for. At first, these newly immigrated peoples were subject to the same kinds of negative stereotyping and generalizations that had previously been assigned to the American colonies' first imports - the slaves - and to the same types of slanders that face many of today's Mexican immigrants. Many of these immigrants grouped together to form ethnic communities which still stand in most of America's eastern cities.

Around about 1915, as conflict over seas began to escalate, and the globe's nations marched towards the First World War, the steady stream of European migration slowly began to dry up. And because the global conflict had its roots in Europe, the European lifeline of migrating workers, which had been flooding America's north eastern shores with millions of immigrants since the 1870's, was effectively cut off. The south on the other hand had been suffering through stagnancy since the end of the civil war and the painfully slow moving reconstruction process.

Now, in most abusive relationships, there comes the point when the person on the receiving end will reach their limit, either mentally, physically, or both. It is at this point that the decision must be made to either fight back or remove one's self from the situation. Basically, it boils down to the most basic rule in nature: survival. The same can be said for a group of people in such a situation. And around the turn of the century scores of African-Americans living in the antiquated South decided that enough was enough. Jim Crow and his unrelenting, hate-driven laws had taken their toll. The grandfather clause had effectively disenfranchised would-be African-American voters. Falling cotton prices led to an economic downturn in the South, and agricultural devastation due to the introduction of the ravenous Boll Weevil insects spurred a depression felt by thousands. Mother Nature had also taken her toll as floods devastated numerous African-American owned properties along the Mississippi river. For many African-Americans it was time to start searching for greener pastures.

Very quickly the northern heads of industry realized that there lay an untapped and extremely willing resource of both trained and unskilled workers virtually wilting away in the South: the American Negro. Northern industrial giants such as the Pennsylvania Railroad Company, Carnegie Steel, and the Ford Company, wasted no time in advertising their abundance of job opportunities. And before you know it, the slow trickle of able bodied Black men heading north broke loose and became a flood. The cities which saw the highest influx of new southern workers were, of course, those whose economies were centered on industry: Detroit, Pittsburgh, New York, and Chicago. According to a report from The Schomberg Center for Research in Black Culture:

"In the decade between 1910 and 1920, New York's black population rose by 66%, Chicago's by 148%, Philadelphia's by 500%. Detroit experienced an amazing growth rate of 611%."

(In Motion; the African-American Migration Experience. The Schomberg Center for Research in Black Culture)

As one might expect, all these new faces and able bodies weren't exactly enthusiastically welcomed by the current workforce. Facing a new form of Jim Crow in the North, the newly immigrated African-American workers were barred from managerial positions or kept from advancing within the workforce due to many "white-only" company policies. The white workforce also blamed the African-American worker for the declining standards of the work environment. As you can probably imagine, once industry leaders realized they could pay their new workers less and still achieve the same amount of production, or more, they quickly began to slash wages for everyone. And so the snowball effect of lessening work place standards, shrinking salary, and the increase in white unemployment began to wear on the "white" American psyche. And I place the term white in quotations for a reason. Once more in this country's history, here is a point in time where the *construction of race* plays a pivotal and important role in determining who is and who isn't.

As black people, or negroes, began to infiltrate the workforce and living spaces of America's urban and industrial northern cities, the Caucasian majority, including the newly immigrated European contingencies of these cities, began to unify in an *us* against *them* mentality. During this time period in particular, differences between Italian, Polish, Russian, German, etc., while still very deeply ingrained in the consciousness of northern American society, begin to diminish in importance. Instead, the new focus of "American" hatred was concentrated on how the new influx of black people negatively affected the living standards of "white people"; a term that would come to incorporate all people not of African, Hispanic, or Asian decent. Again, we have the reemergence of the *negro problem.*

Once this new bond of "whiteness" was cemented, and the unification of newly immigrated European peoples with their "pure-bred" white American brethren was agreed upon, even if only subconsciously, the next step to take in defense of the white community would be the exclusion of the black invaders. It is around this time that the greater Caucasian community, along with the help of the civil government and financial institutions they controlled, developed the pattern and practice of what would come to be known as 'redlining'. Redlining is widely defined as a discriminatory city planning practice by which banks, insurance companies, and similar institutions, refuse or limit loans, mortgages, insurance, and the advertisement of such opportunities, within specific geographic areas, particularly with relation to inner-city neighborhoods.

During this time period white property-owners, banks, and city governments colluded together to concentrate the African-American population into the most dilapidated and undesirable housing available within Northern cities. African-Americans were left with virtually no alternative other than the cramped and destitute living spaces carved out for them. Businesses either vacated their locations within African-American communities, or intentionally destroyed their properties with the intent of collecting insurance monies, adding to the blight of these resource starved neighborhoods.

....

*Let's take time out at this point to underline the importance of this period in our history, for this is the birth of the circumstances which have crafted the – predominantly African-American and Hispanic/Latino - communities that we so easily classify as ghettoes today!

Racial Redlining, although outlawed several decades ago, is a practice which is still implemented to this very day!!! As PhD. Amy Hillier states in her report entitled *Redlining in Philadelphia*, "The word 'redlining' was coined in the late 1960's by community activists in Chicago and was made illegal by the Fair Housing Act of 1968."

As Dr. Hillier explains, the Home Owners' Loan Corporation (HOLC) began a survey of 239 US cities in 1935, and from this survey the HOLC produced color-coded "residential security maps" which indicated the level of security for real estate investments in those cities. A year prior to that, in 1934, the Federal Housing Administration (FHA) which was brought about to insure mortgage lenders, produced an Underwriting Manual as a guide for lenders which utilized "highly racialized neighborhood standards" that lenders were to follow if they intended to do business with the FHA.

Furthermore, a more recent study conducted by the publicly funded Geographic Information Systems (GIS) for Equitable and Sustainable Communities organization, focused on 16 large metropolitan areas in the US and identified "49 major mortgage lenders whose geographic lending patterns, in 62 separate instances, substantially excluded or under-served minority neighborhoods." The patterns studied in this report occurred within the timeframe of 1990-1991.

The study identifies the five major Federal Agencies that oversee Fair Lending policy enforcement as the:

- U.S. Department of Housing and Urban Development (HUD)
- Office of Thrift Supervision
- Controller of the Currency
- Federal Reserve Board

- Federal Deposit Insurance Corporation.

More importantly, the study concludes that, "even though racial redlining has been prohibited by federal civil rights laws for many years, federal authorities have failed to adopt effective regulations and enforcement procedures, thereby condoning both the serious and subtle injuries to minority neighborhoods. *This is a systemic failure.*"

There goes that term again, "systemic", or systematic. A quick refresher: in our earlier discussion of the basics, I defined 'Systematic Oppression' as the *systematically maintained inequality of bargaining power, resulting in one party's lack of ability to negotiate or exercise meaningful choice*. Just thought this was a good point to refresh your memory.

If you're wondering what a GIS is (because I wondered what it was), it is defined as a tool which "integrates hardware, software, and data for capturing, managing, analyzing, and displaying all forms of geographically referenced information", according to the GIS website (www.gis.com). More to the point, it's the tool that Federal and Local Planning committees, banks, and mortgage companies use to process and analyze information about specific areas, when making important business and planning decisions that will affect said areas. You can think of it as a multilayered topographical spreadsheet which displays natural resource, industrial, economic development, law enforcement, education, and ethnic zoning, among other things.

But I digress…Back to the turn of the 20th century (the early 1900's)

....

To summarize the Great Migration, around the start of the
First World War when the steady influx of millions of European
peoples abruptly came to a halt right as the U.S. intended to ramp
up its industrial production of war materials, there was really only
one place the industrious North could turn to solve its labor
shortage. The *where,* the North turned to, was the South. But more
importantly, the *who,* were the African-Americans of the South.
And so, industry sent recruiters and willing and able-bodied
workers responded in droves. Within a decade they had more than
quadrupled the African-American populations in some Northern
cities; the most populated of which being Detroit, Chicago, and
New York.

The Great Migration not only brought a tremendous influx of
able and willing African-American workers to the industrious
north, it also produced an extremely talented contingent of writers,
artists, musicians, and actors. The Harlem borough of New York
City would become the heart of the cultural rebirth within the
community. From this epicenter, writers and intellectuals such as
Langston Hughes, Zora Neale Hurston, and W.E.B. Dubois would
send shockwaves throughout not only Black America, but
throughout Mainstream America and Europe as well. For the first
time in this country's history we would see the evolution of an
African-American middle-class; a Black bourgeoisie that would
later come to be known, thanks to W.E.B. Dubois himself, as The
Talented Tenth – the "top 10%" of the African-American race
whose duty it would be to reach down and lift up as many of the
masses as it possibly could.

In response to this new and alarming growth of not only the
African-American communities in *their* cities, workplaces, and
neighborhoods, but also in response to this newfound sense of
pride and entitlement within the African-American consensus,

America's newest European immigrants joined forces with America's oldest European immigrants to form the bond of white brotherhood which would work to ensure that the new Black populace was reminded of its place in American society. As Hughes, Kroehler, and Vander Zander explain, "In the view of Realistic Group Conflict theory, when the interests of groups coincide, intergroup attitudes will be relatively positive. However, if the interests of the groups diverge, as is the case when groups compete for scarce resources such as land, jobs, or power, negative prejudicial attitudes will result."

What followed were shady lending and zoning practices institutionalized by city planners, banks, mortgage companies, and landlords which conspired not only to keep blacks out of white neighborhoods, but also to keep much needed resources away from these communities such as grocery stores, restaurants and businesses. When African-Americans were able to find housing, slumlords maximized profits by subdividing tenements which were already overflowing with families into even smaller living spaces. The result of too many people living in the same space, stacked on top of each other, with limited resources, coupled with the frustration of facing constant societal and workplace degradation, is a situation which has all the familiar symptoms of a ghetto. And speaking of symptoms, this is the point in history when the African-American community begins to become inversely affected by serious health issues such as asthma, diabetes, and infant-death rates. Cramped living spaces, poorly ventilated workplaces, and segregated hospitals did little to ensure the good health of Black people. Indeed, this was the beginning of the social experiment that is the African-American ghetto in America.

Race Riots

For those of us over the age of 25, the term riot probably conjures up images of a city engulfed in flames, rampant violence, looting, and general chaos. More than likely, the video footage of four LAPD officers brutally beating motorist Rodney King replays over and over in your thoughts. And even more likely, for most of us at least, the 1992 Los Angeles riots are the most vibrant and tangible example of how volatile a combination the mixture of racial tension, social injustice, and anger can be.

For those of us just a generation older, you may even recall the 1964 Watts Riots. Interestingly enough, both riots were sparked by a law enforcement altercation with an African-American motorist, but were truly the result of years, decades, and centuries worth of mistreatment, degradation, poverty, and injustice.

More recently, perhaps you're reminded of the fatal Police shooting of a young African-American male by the name of Oscar Grant, III, and the reactionary –although miniscule- riots that swept through Oakland, CA the very first week of January, 2009 -a situation in which the Caucasian officer who shot Grant in the early morning hours of the New Year, was not arrested, and simply refused to cooperate with investigators until he was apprehended January 13 in Nevada, and had to be extradited back to California.

And now be honest, when you first read the word riot, did the images in your mind depict angry, violent, and most likely poor inner-city minorities as the aggressors? Be honest. And don't be ashamed if those are the images that first *raced* through your mind, because thanks to the media those are the most relevant and repeated images that American society is able to reference whenever a conversation turns to the topic of riots or general civil unrest. All alliteration aside, the American public would be well served to be reminded of the fact that less than 100 years ago, around the turn of the century, the angry mobs which provoked several of this country's deadliest and most devastating riots were White.

These conflicts were almost uniformly the result of white fear of a growing black populace, or consciousness, within a given community. And although these altercations spanned a period of nearly 45 years (from 1898 – 1943), the most serious incidents occurred around the end of the First World War (around 1918). It was during this time that African-Americans were filling the gaps in the Northern industrial workforce created by the departure of America's young white males-turned soldiers. It was during this time that African-American soldiers who had been overseas and fought for this country just like the rest of their American military brethren, were returning home and demanding, heaven forbid, a little dignity and respect. (Robert Gibson. The Negro Holocaust: Yale-New Haven Teachers Institute. 2008) The most brutal and bloody time period in domestic American history besides the Civil War, and perhaps the most senseless, was the summer of 1919, otherwise known as The Red Summer. In 1919 alone, there were 26 Race Riots on record; in cities large and small, north and south, and all throughout the nation. The riots of that year would take the lives of *over one hundred African-Americans, and leave several thousands injured and homeless* – in 1919 alone!

Now, let's not make the grave mistake of trivializing these events. I understand that it is hard to grasp the severity and impact of these events in today's overly-stimulated and violence-numb society; a society in which video games, movies, and daily newscasts have inundated our senses with visions of death and destruction to the point that we are no longer able to react. However, if for only a moment, I ask that you take the time to truly conceptualize how frightening it must have been to be a person of color at this moment in American history. Imagine being a young Black man living with the knowledge - not to be confused with the acceptance - of the fact that you are not to defend yourself if attacked, for fear of retaliation visited tenfold upon your family and your community. Imagine, if you can, how powerless and infuriating that must have felt. Imagine the hatred and contempt that a circumstance like that would breed within you. Picture yourself as a young African-American woman living in a society where the men in your life, those who should be the protector and provider for you and your family, could be the random target of mob violence at any given time. Imagine your home, your community and your life, in a constant state of fear and uncertainty. How would you maintain your sanity? How could you maintain your focus?

Emmitt Till's legacy; enough is enough

August 28, 1955 is a day that will forever exist in infamy in America's storied history (even if most of us have forgotten its importance), for it is on that day that young 14 year old Emmett Till was kidnapped from his uncle's home in Money, Mississippi, and brutally beaten and killed by J.W. Milam and Roy Bryant, as punishment for flirting with Bryant's wife Carolyn; a white woman. The grotesque image of Till's disfigured corpse is emblazoned upon the memory of anyone old enough to remember this moment in our country's history. As are the smiling faces of his indignant and defiant murderer's upon hearing the news that they had been acquitted of the charges against them. So boastful and proud of their actions were Milam and Bryant, that they openly discussed the details of Till's murder to reporter William Bradford Huie, only one year later. In his recount of how defiant, unafraid, and most likely unaware, young Emmett Till had been in the face of death, Milam stated:

"We were never able to scare him. They had just filled him so full of that poison that he was hopeless… Well, what else could we do? He was hopeless. I'm no bully; I never hurt a nigger in my life. I like niggers -- in their place -- I know how to work 'em. But I just decided it was time a few people got put on notice. As long as I live and can do anything about it, niggers are gonna stay in their place. Niggers ain't gonna vote where I live. If they did, they'd control the government. They ain't gonna go to school with my kids. And when a nigger gets close to mentioning sex with a white woman, he's tired o' livin'. I'm likely to kill him. Me and my folks fought for this country, and we got some rights. I stood there in that shed and listened to that nigger throw that poison at me, and I just made up my mind. 'Chicago boy,' I said, 'I'm tired of 'em sending your kind down here to stir up trouble. Goddam you, I'm going to make an example of you -- just so everybody can know how me and my folks stand."

- William Bradford Huie. "The Shocking Story of Approved Killing in Mississippi". Look Magazine; 1956"

As disturbingly evil and gut-wrenching as Milam and Bryant's actions may have been, the decision of Till's mother,

Mamie Till, to conduct an open casket funeral service for her son may have been equally as brilliant. I say this because I believe that it was the nationally circulated images of Till's corpse, and the reactions they caused, far and wide, amongst white and black, which truly galvanized and set the Civil Rights Movement in motion.

Once Black America came to the realization that inaction in the face of such atrocities would do nothing but ensure the occurrence of more heinous and vicious attacks, leaders within the community decided that enough was enough. In my opinion, Emmitt Till's death was the straw that broke the camel's back. Within 100 days of his brutal murder, in an orchestrated move on behalf of African-American leaders in Montgomery, Alabama, Mrs. Rosa Parks took a stand against inequality by refusing to stand and vacate her seat for a white man on the city's public transportation. Five days later Dr. Martin Luther King, Jr. was appointed as the President of the Montgomery Improvement Association, and the Civil Rights Movement was underway.

....

The Big Picture

The Great Depression

- o On "Black" Tuesday, October 29, 1929, the stock market crashed, signaling the worst economic crash in recorded history.
- o The Great Depression, a time period of severe unemployment and inflation, would last for nearly 10 years; hitting poor and minority populations the hardest.
- o Franklin Delano Roosevelt's New Deal Programs, a series of stimulus packages for the economy and workforce, would breathe new life into the American economy.

McCarthyism and the Communist scare:

- o Brought on by Republican Senator Joseph McCarthy, of Wisconsin, and spurred by the very real but also very exaggerated prospect of Communist infiltration in America, the term "McCarthyism" refers to the "witch-hunt" approach of the United States government, to flush out so-called "card carrying Communists"; which oddly enough were mostly artists and writers, or anyone else brave enough to question the activities of the American Government.
- o McCarthyism, although now widely regarded as misdirected propaganda efforts, distorted the livelihood of several hundred Americans during the 1940's and 50's.

....

Chapter 3

The Golden Era

The turn of the 20th Century was a pivotal moment in American history, and a tumultuous time period for the rest of the world. Within the first half of the millennium there were not one, but two World Wars. Two conflicts of such mythic proportions that nearly every reach of civilization on the globe was impacted in some way. After Germany's defeat and deconstruction in the aftermath of World War I, Adolf Hitler would rebuild the country upon a platform of race propaganda; Arian supremacy against perceived Jewish inferiority. And after a prolonged Nazi political campaign of degradation and terror, one of the most heinous and unforgivable events in human history would ensue with the Holocaust, and the loss of over 6 million Jewish lives. The birth of the Atomic bomb, developed in the Manhattan Project, would mean the instant death of hundreds of thousands of Japanese in the blasts of Hiroshima and Nagasaki, in 1945, as a response to the attacks on the American Naval base at Pearl Harbor. All the while domestically, America would be forced to deal with a sizeable demographic shift in the form of the Great Migration, and all of the repercussions associated with it; urban red-lining, lynching, race riots, etc. Brown skinned peoples of African, Latin, and Asian descent rightfully feared for their lives in every American city on the map.

And so it is with all of this in mind, that when we look at the ghettos of today, and when we are psycho-analyzing the mind-state of the millions and millions of Americans living in ghetto-like conditions, we must not forget the less-than-a-century-old circumstances which have shaped and perpetuated the realities of inner-city urban, and even suburban life. When the conversation turns towards the subject of African-American mistrust of law enforcement let us not forget that for most of this country's history the African-American community has been the victim of police brutality, intolerance, and indifference; and to this day the community is still subject to random police aggression. When the conversation turns towards the lack of African-American participation in politics, let us not forget the fact that excluding perhaps the last 40-50 years of this country's existence, most of the political policies concerning the African-American community, or any minority group for that matter, have been ineffective or outright ignored. In more recent times, most of the policies which could have proven beneficial for underserved communities have been overturned; take Affirmative Action, *which actually did more for White females than any other group*, for example. Most of the African-American community has tuned itself out to politics because it somewhat rightfully feels that, as the *Rage Against The Machine* song ("Killing in the Name of") says, "Some of those that run forces, are the same that burn crosses." That said, it is to be noted that the mere presence of Barack Obama has created a palpable resurgence in African-American political interest.

And when considering the educational realities of inner-city and poor areas, let us not forget the very real and substantial impact of the red-lining policies began in the 1900's, and the fact that in our current system, state and local funds account for about 90% of educational expenditures in this country; with the major sources of state funds being local sales and income taxes on the personal and corporate levels, including property taxes. And if this is the case, then communities which have been historically redlined are doomed to suffer from insufficient funding due to the fact that property values are inherently inferior in comparison to their neighbors. So even when the decision of Brown vs. the Board of Education came down in 1954 - which was actually the culmination of several multi-racial discrimination cases going on at the time - *legally* ending the practice and implementation of separate but equal public facilities, publicly funded schooling was still inherently unequal.

For nearly 100 years, from the mid-1860's to the 1960's, the African-American community was subjected to numerous half-measures and empty edicts bellowed from the halls of Washington, as well as the victims of heinous hate crimes, lynching, racially charged massacres, and acts of prejudice from the greater American community. For nearly a century after African-Americans were supposedly 'free' in this country, we were subjected to violence, unfair treatment, degradation, and death whenever we tried to utilize the supposed rights inherent to citizens of this country. This is the understanding -not the excuse- which must frame any type of discussion about the current state of the African-American community in this country.

Personally, when I consider the totality of our lifespan in America, I refer to the 1960's, and especially the *early* Civil Rights period, as the Golden Era of the African-American zeitgeist in this country. Spurred by centuries worth of anger and resentment, the fear of continued and escalating violence, fueled by pride, a sense of righteousness, and an overwhelming desire to be treated and seen as equals, the Black people of this country finally decided that this would be the moment in which they stood against it all. It is during this time period that the African-American community finally begins to assemble - in mass movements - behind two polarized leaders: Dr. Martin Luther King Jr. and his passive, 'non-violent' preaching, and the self-empowering, militant Malcolm "X" and the Nation of Islam.

And even though the tactical and philosophical positions of the leaders were drastically different, their underlying goals were similar: unity, respect, and equality within the African-American community and for the African-American community. During this period, for the first time in the mainstream media at least, there is coverage of African-American leaders and their messages- and all across the country there begins to form cohesiveness amongst the community around a common concept: equality and basic human rights. For the first time in this country's history, we are beginning to find our voice. We are beginning to mobilize. We are beginning to unite.

Malcolm

Malcolm X will forever and always be remembered and revered in the African-American community; even if mainstream America seems resolved to omit him from the history books. He will always hold a special place in our hearts and our consciousness, a place reserved for only our best and brightest. Reviled by the media, and feared by most of mainstream America due to his characterization as 'the angriest Negro in America', Malcolm was respected the world over for his audacity to speak to white America as no black or brown person had dared to before. If we were Cuban, he would have been our Che Guevara (although Che was actually Argentinean); our fearless freedom fighter, ready and willing to lay down his life for the sake of his people. He was a man who cared not for important sounding positions or titles -an individual truly devoted to the enlightenment and liberation of his people! In my life, he has been the single most influential male role model next to my father. In our history as a people, no one before him, and no one after him, has been as brazen, as eloquent, or as heartfelt a speaker and champion of the cause of Black people in America. Martin Luther King, Jr. was without doubt an extremely educated and eloquent speaker. No one can question the integrity of his ideas or the sincerity of his words, but the fierceness, the blunt reality, and the passion in the messaging of the demand for respect, is Malcolm's alone.

His story is remarkable, and the definition of a life spent learning. Sentenced at age 21 to 8 to 10 years in prison, in 1946, after a life of poverty, struggle, and the highs and lows of street hustle, Malcolm would serve 6 ½ years in 3 federal prisons before his release in 1952. While incarcerated, Malcolm was introduced to the Nation of Islam (NOI) and the teachings of the Honorable Elijah Muhammad. Within the time span of 10 years, Malcolm X, who by then had become the Nations' second in command, and most feared and respected representative to the outside world, had elevated the NOI from a small grassroots organization to a level of national prominence and relevance never before achieved by an all-Black organization. Towards the end of that tenure, through the ugly combination of jealousy, internal politics (never engaged in by Malcolm himself), and documented government interference, Malcolm was on the outs with the Nation. By 1963, Malcolm was a man with a target on his back and a price on his head; both literally and figuratively.

In Malcolm's last few years, he would once again experience an intellectual and ideological revolution. Stepping away from the NOI and taking the pilgrimage to the Holy city of Mecca -that every able-bodied and economically-able Muslim strives to experience- Malcolm would come to see the short-comings inherent in some of the Nations teachings. His experience in the Holy land would open his eyes to the true unity to be found in the Muslim religion, regardless of ones skin tone. Through his encounters with world leaders and intellectuals, rich, poor, white, black and every shade in between during his time abroad, he would come to such revelations as this:

"American society makes it next to impossible for humans to meet in America and not be conscious of their color differences… It isn't the American white man who is (naturally) a racist, but it is the American political, economic, and social atmosphere that automatically nourishes a racist psychology in the white man."

And although his message would continue to be very ethnocentric upon his return to the states, no longer was he as exclusionary as before; as the Nation had molded him to be. As Malcolm wrote in letters to friends and family members while on his religious journey, "I've had enough of someone else's propaganda… I'm for truth, no matter who tells it. I'm for justice, no matter who it is for or against. I'm a human being first and foremost, and as such I'm for whoever and whatever benefits humanity as a whole." (Malcolm X; Alex Haley. The Autobiography of Malcolm X. The Random House Publishing Group: New York, 1973)

Born in Omaha, Nebraska on May 19, 1925, Malcolm Little, who would come to be known the world over as Malcolm X, and later as El-Hajj Malik El-Shabazz to his closest associates, was gunned down in Harlem's Audubon Ballroom on February 21, 1965. The men accused of planning and carrying out the assassination were reportedly members of the Nation of Islam. Controversy still shrouds the circumstances surrounding Malcolm's death, but his legacy as one of the most impassioned and audacious leaders that our community has ever seen will forever remain intact.

"I am only facing the facts when I know that any moment of any day, or any night, could bring me death… I know that societies often have killed the people who have helped to change those societies. And if I can die having brought any light, having exposed any meaningful truth that will help to destroy the racist cancer that is malignant in the body of America – then, all of the credit is due to Allah. Only the mistakes have been mine."

- Malcolm X, 1965

Martin

If Malcolm was our Che Guevara, then Martin was our Mahatma Gandhi. And while I have always been drawn to the fiery disposition, and most readily identified with the embattled but enlightened journey of Malcolm X, I have simultaneously admired the teachings of Dr. Martin Luther King, Jr. Although admittedly, this admiration has come from afar. For whatever reason, there has always been somewhat of a disconnect for me. And I believe that for the most part that disconnect has been the product of misunderstanding. Misunderstanding in the sense that it is hard for me to fathom such restraint in the face of such peril; such unrestrained and unprovoked hatred. How does one find the resolve to continually turn the other cheek? How does one preach non-violence in the apex of such violent times? I must admit that I have been guilty of mistaking strategy for cowardice, non-violence for fear of rebuke. How does one find the reserve as Martin once did, and as Obama now attempts to, to sit down face to face with ones enemy and begin to work toward resolution?

Coupled with that misunderstanding was a deep-seated uncertainty. I have always been cursed with the need to question things; the desire to understand the real message behind what is being said - the implied versus the stated. And in the case of Martin Luther King Jr., and the amount of, and *slant* of the publicity he received during his lifetime, as opposed to say that of Malcolm X and the Nation of Islam, there was always –for me at least- a lingering suspicion of a house negro/field negro situation. And even now, as I say those words, I fight a knee-jerk reaction because I know the exact sentiment that that sentence will spark in most. "But you're African-American, aren't you supposed to love Martin Luther King?!?" And quite honestly, that is exactly my point. We *were supposed to* love him. We were supposed to agree with and fall in line with his non-violent, compliant approach to solving the issues of inequality. We were supposed to quietly accept the brutalities and the beatings, the humiliations and the indignities, all the while hoping and praying for a better day. That's exactly what *they* wanted. And for a while, I mistakenly aligned Dr. King's tactics with complicity to White agendas.

As we will cover shortly, government officials actually referred to King's position as *"obedience to white liberal doctrine",* and they considered him no real threat unless he were to abandon that stance in favor of a more militant one. The government and media of the 1960's positioned King and his followers as the model Negros going about things in the model way, as where in comparison, Malcolm X and the NOI – with their do for yourself, protect yourself doctrine – were portrayed as the enemy; and in Malcolm's case, as public enemy number one. That never sat well with me. And I mistakenly and wrongly wrote King and his tactics off because of it. I say again here that I was mistaken in doing this, and more than that, I was flat out wrong. The media played its games and tried its hardest to manipulate the situation, but the messages of both Martin and Malcolm had merit. In reality they needed each other in order to give teeth to their respective stances. They needed each other as Black needs White, or as North needs South. Once again, it is the concept of complementing opposites; the yin and the yang. Non-violence poses no real problem and elicits no response if there is never the threat of violence - the threat of retaliation. On the flip side of that coin, violence only begets more violence, which is a path that leads to destruction. Martin and Malcolm created a delicate balance and together spearheaded a movement which could not be ignored.

I often think back to the 1960's and wonder if I could have survived in such a turbulent time. Could I have turned the other cheek after that cheek had been spit on or struck? Or would I have been lynched after defending my pride and dignity as a man and a protector of my own? I think of the tremendous physical and mental weight of the period, and wonder if I would have been able to withstand the pressure. I do not know if I will ever find the answers to those questions. And I am optimistic that I will never in my lifetime be forced to. The basis of that hope stems from the grateful acknowledgement that a man who lived only two generations before me did have the courage and fortitude necessary to answer those questions. And that man's name, was Dr. Martin Luther King, Jr.; born January 15, 1929, in Atlanta, GA, to Reverend and Mrs. Martin Luther King.

In direct contrast to the upbringing of Malcolm "X" Little, Martin Luther King, Jr. was born into a comfortable and stable middle-class suburban home. As where Malcolm's father was versed in the separatist 'back to Africa' rhetoric of Marcus Garvey, King was brought up in the teachings and philosophies of the Christian church. As where Malcolm's formal education ended in his middle school years, Martin's would conclude when he received his PhD. in Systematic Theology from Boston University, at the age of 26.

Almost immediately upon entering adulthood, King was thrust into the front lines of the Civil Rights battlefield. The year 1955 was a very busy time period for King. Not only would he receive his doctorate degree, but he would also welcome the birth of his first child, as well as take on the role of President of the Montgomery Improvement Association. After the arrest of Mrs. Rosa Parks, King would lead a successful, although hotly contested, year long boycott of the Montgomery bus system. Two years later he would become President of the newly formed Southern Christian Leadership Conference (SCLC). (James Melvin Washington. I Have A Dream: Harper Collins Publishers, 1992) The next chapter of King's life would be a steady succession of marches, demonstrations, speeches, sit-ins, jailings, court cases, and attempts on the lives of both Martin and his family, including one nearly successful stabbing in Harlem the fall of 1958.

King's biggest inspiration in his non-violent approach to civil rights attainment was the former Indian lawyer and activist, Mahatma Gandhi. In 1959 he and his wife would spend a month in India studying the teachings of Gandhi. Although King had always been a proponent of achieving equality through peaceful and legal means, I believe it is at this point, while in the heart of India, and through his study of Gandhi's tactical approach to equality, that King would begin to cement his strategic stance. As he explains in his now famous "Letter from a Birmingham Jail":

"Nonviolent direct action seeks to create such a crises and establish such creative tension that a community that has constantly refused to negotiate is forced to confront the issue. It seeks so to dramatize the issue that it can no longer be ignored...The purpose of direct action is to create a situation so crisis-packed that it will inevitably open the door to negotiation." (James Melvin Washington. I Have A Dream: Harper Collins Publishers, 1992)

Martin Luther King, Jr. would reach a world renowned level of notoriety, and in 1963, on the steps of the Lincoln Memorial in Washington D.C., he would deliver one of the World's most famous oratories in the form of his "I Have a Dream" speech. And at age 35, he would become the youngest ever Nobel Peace Prize recipient.

King's legacy is a litany of legal battles and Civil Rights victories, insightful words and remarkable actions. He was an inspiration to both Black and White, Latino and Asian, young and old. A year before his death, the Justice Department reported that in the southern states of Mississippi, Georgia, Alabama, Louisiana, and South Carolina, over half (50%) of all eligible African-American voters were registered; a figure that can definitely be attributed in part to the work of Dr. Martin Luther King, Jr., amongst others. On April 4, 1968, the world lost one of its most influential human rights activists at the hands of an assassin. I find it not so coincidental that Martin's death came at a time when he was beginning to critique the American government more harshly than he had ever previously done. As ordained Baptist Minister and present day African-American intellectual Michael Eric Dyson offers, if Dr. Martin Luther King, Jr. were alive today Reverend Jeremiah Wright might not be the only person Senator Obama would have to distance himself from. Martin Luther King, Jr. was well versed in Liberation Theology, and towards the end of his life his sermons were growing more and more critical of America's political and social system. One might be so inclined to make the assumption that his turn in rhetorical direction may have been the impetus for his assassination. I still find it interesting that both Martin and Malcolm were the victims of assassination even as they were under the ever watchful guise of federal government surveillance. But I digress.

Although Martin and Malcolm traveled down varying paths, and rose to prominence through differing ideologies, towards the end of their lives their vision was the same; equality, respect, and justice for all. Their lives are, to me, the definition of courage; the willingness to do whatever is necessary for the betterment of others, even when faced with the knowledge that it will cost the ultimate sacrifice - your life. That is a leader. That is the kind of individual that I would willingly follow into any battle.

The Black Civil Rights Movement , a time period reaching from the mid 1950's well in to the late 1960's, was a miraculous moment in the history of Black people in this country. It was a time of great danger. It was a time of much civil unrest, violence, and fear. It was a time of change. This time period was critical in the formation of a Black consciousness in this country. Never before had the Black peoples of this country achieved such levels of notoriety, or reached such levels of unity. The Black Civil Rights Movement was the culmination of centuries worth of degradation, disgrace, and death. It was the moment in time when the entire community decided that enough was enough.

Organization was the hallmark of the time, and religion was the all powerful organizer. Whether it was behind the non-violent Christian teachings of black churches, which urged their followers to adhere to the peaceful and passive preaching of Jesus Christ, or whether it was through the active and militant order of the Nation of Islam – which promoted self-empowering methods in order to strengthen the community, among other things - the Black people of America found strength in their growing unity. In either corner, one would hear the familiar chorus of equality, dignity, and respect. In either corner, one would find dedicated and passionate followers.

I refer to the Black Civil Rights Movement as the Golden Era for Black people in this country, because it is during this time period - for the first time in this nation's history - that the Black people of this country collectively decided to become more than just black people, and make an unwavering stand to become Americans! A statement made loud and proud for the whole world to hear. "Say it loud. I'm Black and I'm proud!" (James Brown) A statement for which the American government would certainly have a response.

··

The Big Picture

Immigration Act of 1965

o counterpart to Civil Rights Act of 1964
o abolished quotas of 1924
o *set stage for large influx of Asian and Latin American immigration*
o Approximately 23 million immigrants entered the country between the years 1966 and 2000. (Roger Daniels. "The Immigration Act of 1965". America.gov: April 3, 2008)

··

Chapter 4

The Empire Strikes Back

For as long as there have been Black people in this country there has been government interest in Black people; interest inasmuch as an overseer-slave type of relationship. Interest in solving *the Negro problem*. Obviously, slavery was as profitable for this country as any worker-employer relationship could possibly be. This nation's original cash crop was cotton, and thanks to the original Africans that inhabited these lands this nation made quite a pretty penny in cotton production. In today's society that accumulation of wealth is referred to as "old money"- and there are plenty of old money families still thriving. In today's America, first generation and "illegal" Hispanic and Latino peoples have taken on the role of America's slave laborers. They have taken on the role of working for little or next to nothing. They are the ones willing to do whatever it takes to eek out a living in this great land. Let me remind you that this is a country built on the notion of 'free labor'; built on the backs, blood, sweat, and tears of the unfortunate. So don't mind me if I laugh at the mainstream uproar over illegal aliens entering this country. That pipeline of cheap labor is the last thing this country wants cutoff. And believe me, the 'powers that be' know that. But I digress.

Once the African slaves were freed, the nations' interest in Black people became twofold; in the North, negroes were a vital contingent of the industrial workforce and the urban cityscape, while in the South, their presence served more to maintain the societal norms which had been established by the institution of slavery. But once the negroes of this country decided that they were tired of simply being negroes, and once they collectively decided that they too deserved to have some share in the bounty and promises of this land – in essence, once they resolved to become more than generationally removed Africans in this country, make a stand against intolerance and cruelty - and become African-*Americans*, the government's interest in the Black people of this country took a markedly different and more sinister turn.

COINTELPRO, or the Counter Intelligence Program, refers to a series of United States Government funded operations run by the FBI from 1956-1971; the key years in the development of the Civil Rights Movement. As is reported by Attorney Paul Wolf, its main purpose was to investigate, disrupt, and ultimately destroy "politically dissident" organizations; which basically meant all Civil Rights Movements.

Paul Wolf is a Washington, D.C. based attorney who specializes in Human and Civil Rights, Criminal Defense, International Law, and Freedom of Information Act cases. The following information comes directly from a website he has dedicated to publicizing the operations of Cointelpro. This information in particular focuses on the Cointelpros which concentrated on "Black Nationalist Hate Groups":

An introduction to the program –

The purpose of this new counterintelligence endeavor is to expose, disrupt, misdirect, discredit, or otherwise neutralize the activities of black nationalist, hate-type organizations and groupings, their leadership, spokesmen, membership, and supporters, and to counter their propensity for violence and civil disorder.

… Efforts of the various groups to consolidate their forces or to recruit new or youthful adherents must be frustrated. No opportunity should be missed to exploit through counterintelligence techniques the organizational and personal conflicts of the leaderships of the groups and where possible an effort should be made to capitalize upon existing conflicts between competing black nationalist organizations. When an opportunity is apparent to disrupt or neutralize black nationalist, hate-type organizations through the cooperation of established local news media contacts or through such contact with sources available to the Seat of Government, in every instance careful attention must be given to the proposal to insure the targeted group is disrupted, ridiculed, or discredited through the publicity and not merely publicized.

The following is a communication from the Director of COINTELPRO sent to 23 field offices on Aug. 26, 1967:

The Counterintelligence Program is now being expanded to include 41 offices. ... For maximum effectiveness of the Counterintelligence Program, and to prevent wasted effort, long range goals are being set.

1. Prevent the coalition of militant Black Nationalist groups. In unity there is strength; a truism that is no less valid for all its triteness.

2. Prevent the rise of a "messiah" who could unify, and electrify, the militant black nationalist movement. Malcolm

X might have been such a "messiah;" he is the martyr of the movement today. Martin Luther King, Stokely Carmichael and Elijah Muhammed all aspire to this position. Elijah Muhammed is less of a threat because of his age. King could be a very real contender for this position should he abandon his supposed "obedience" to "white, liberal doctrines" (nonviolence) and embrace black nationalism. Carmichael has the necessary charisma to be a real threat in this way.

3. Prevent violence on the part of black nationalist groups... Through counterintelligence it should be possible to pinpoint potential troublemakers and neutralize them before they exercise their potential for violence.

4. Prevent militant black nationalist groups and leaders from gaining respectability, by discrediting them to three separate segments of the community. The goal of discrediting black nationalists must be handled tactically in three ways. You must discredit these groups and individuals to, first, the responsible Negro community. Second, they must be discredited to the white community, both the responsible community and to "liberals" who have vestiges of sympathy for militant black nationalists simply because they are Negroes. Third, these groups must be discredited in the eyes of Negro radicals, the followers of the movement. This last area requires entirely different tactics from the first two. Publicity about violent tendencies and radical statements merely enhances black nationalists to the last group; it adds "respectability" in a different way.

5. A final goal should be to prevent the long-range growth of militant black nationalist organizations, especially among youth. Specific tactics to prevent these groups from converting young people must be developed.

*Important occurrences to keep in mind with respect to the timeframe of COINTELPRO operations (1956-71):

- Malcolm X is assassinated in Feb of 1965
- The Black Panther Party is founded in Oct of 1966
- Martin Luther King, Jr. is assassinated in April of 1968

In the early 1970's, the United States Senate commissioned a Select Committee to study and report on the policies and procedures of intelligence activities conducted by U.S. government agencies as they pertained to American citizens. One of the committees' base findings was that "the unexpressed major premise of much of COINTELPRO is that the Bureau (FBI) has a role in *maintaining the existing social order*, and that its efforts should be aimed toward combating those who threaten that order." In essence, if one were to make the argument that there were significant issues of societal inequality present in American society during the time period of the late 1950's to early 1970's, then the report conducted by the U.S. Senate found enough substantial evidence to make the claim that government agencies actively and fervently worked against the improvement of social standing and progress for the oppressed peoples of this country.

And in April of 1976, a substantial and detailed report on the actions of those agencies was produced. The following is a compilation of specific examples of COINTELPRO actions taken against individuals, groups, or entire organizations, utilizing the techniques specified by the agency.

"You can trace (the origins of Cointelpro techniques) up and back to foreign intelligence, particularly penetration of the group by the individual informant. Before you can engage in counterintelligence you must have intelligence...If you have good intelligence and know what (an organization) is going to do, you can seed distrust, sow misinformation."

  - George Moore, Racial Intelligence Section supervisor of the Black Nationalist COINTELPRO

COINTELPRO techniques:

1) Propaganda, or the use of "friendly" media contacts to promote certain stories

  - The Miami Division developed a source at a local television station and the source produced a news special on black nationalists and on the New Left...Local New Left and black nationalist leaders were interviewed on the show and seemed to have been chosen for either their inability to articulate or their simpering and stupid appearance...Especially important was the choice of individuals interviewed as they did not have the ability to stand up to a professional newsman.
      - Director to 42 field offices, Aug 5, 1968

- "Not long before, I had been on the Jerry Williams radio program in Boston, when someone handed me an item hot off the Associated Press machine. I read that a chapter of the Louisiana Citizens Council had just offered a $10,000 reward for my death."
  - Malcolm X Autobiography, p.339

2) Promote factionalism within or between groups

- These suggestions are to create factionalism between not only the national leaders but also local leaders, steps to neutralize all organizational efforts of the BPP (Black Panther Party) as well as create suspicion concerning their respective spouses and suspicion as to who may be cooperating with law enforcement...
  - G.C. Moore to W.C. Sullivan, Sept 27, 1968

- Over the years considerable thought has been given, and action taken with Bureau approval, relating to methods through which the NOI could be discredited in the eyes of the general black populace or through which factionalism among leadership could be created... Factional disputes have been developed – the most notable being MALCOLM X LITTLE.
  - SAC Chicago to Director, Jan 22, 1969

- Purpose of counterintelligence action is to disrupt BPP (Black Panther Party), and it is immaterial whether facts exist to substantiate the charge.
  - Fragment of memo from Director, Sept 16, 1970

3) The use of hostile third parties against target groups

- "In January, the Police departments of Oakland, Berkeley, and San Francisco unleashed a terror and arrest campaign against the Black Panther Party…sixteen members of our party were arrested gratuitously and charged with offenses that had never been committed."

 - Eldridge Cleaver: Post-Prison Writings and Speeches. A Ramparts Book, Random House, NY, 1969

- Chicago airtel …dated 5/2/68 and captioned "Richard Claxton Gregory" concern a speech by Gregory on 4/28/68 where he noted that "Syndicate hoods are living all over. They are the filthiest snakes that exist on this earth." …Consider the use of this statement in developing a counterintelligence operation to alert La Cosa Nostra (LCN) to Gregory's attack on LCN. It is noted that other speeches by Gregory also contain attacks on the LCN.
                               - Director to SAC Chicago May 15, 1968

4) Disseminating Derogatory Information to family, friends, and associates

- It is suggested that consideration be given to convey the impression that (Stokely) Carmichael is a CIA informant. One method of accomplishing the above would be to have a carbon copy of informant report reportedly written by Carmichael to the CIA carefully deposited in the automobile of a close Black Nationalist friend… It is also suggested that we inform a certain percentage of reliable

criminal and racial informants that "we heard from reliable sources that Carmichael is a CIA agent".
> - Fragment of FBI Memorandum, July 19, 1968

- The Committee requested that the Bureau provide it with a list of any 'COINTELPRO-type' actions since April 28,1971 (the supposed termination date of the operation)...The Committee discovered (an instance where) information on an attorney's political backgournd was furnished to friendly newspaper sources under the so-called "Mass Media Program" intended to discredit both the attorney and his client.

(Final Report of the Select Committee to study Governmental Operations with respect to Intelligence Activities United States Senate. April 23, 1976: Source –www.icdc.com, cited 7/2/2008)

5) Contacts with employers

- In San Diego, an anonymous telephone call to the landlord of the US organization resulted in the group being evicted from its headquarters.
> - G.C. Moore to W.C. Sullivan, May 14, 1970

6) Use and abuse of government processes

- "My case was designated a "special study case", which required that I see my parole agent four times each month. Severe new restrictions were to be imposed. I was not to go outside a seven mile area; specifically, I was not to cross the Bay Bridge. I was to keep my name out of the news for the next six months; specifically, my face was not to appear on any TV screen. I was not to make any more speeches. And I was not to write anything critical of the California Department of Corrections or any California politician...I was told, 'All that Governor Reagan has to do is sign his name on a dotted line and you are dead, with no appeal'."

- Eldridge Cleaver: Post-Prison Writings and Speeches. A Ramparts Book, Random House, NY, 1969

For those of you who still question the capacity of our government to stoop so low, to take actions so strong, so deviant - so unlawful - against its own citizens, let me offer you another voice to consider. Alfred W. McCoy is a professor of History at the University of Wisconsin-Madison. He also happens to be a world renowned expert on the history and politics of Southeast Asia, most notably Vietnam and the Philippines. In an interview with David Barsamian conducted in 1990, Barsamian asked McCoy if the threat of communism, or of losing a strategic territory such as Vietnam to communist ideology, was impetus enough for the government to risk being linked with drug trafficking. McCoy's answer was so shockingly true, so brutally honest, that it almost leaves the reader with a sense of surreal-ness as one attempts to grapple with what they've just heard- it's the kind of thing you hope not to be true. He gave an example of an answer given to him by a high-ranking government official whilst in the middle of conducting his own research in Southeast Asia. According to McCoy, the official laid it out like this:

"When you think about the essential skills it takes to have an extra-legal operation - to have somebody killed, to mobilize a crowd, to do what it does when societies are in flux, when power is unclear and to be grabbed and shaped and molded into a new state - you want to overthrow a government and put a new one in - how do you do it? Who does this? Accountants? - They go to the office everyday. Students? They go to classes - they're good for maybe one riot or something, but they've got to get on to medical school or law or whatever they're doing. Where do you get people who have this kind of skill? You have your own operatives and they're limited. Particularly if you're a foreigner, your capacity to move something in the streets is very limited... Sometimes you can turn to a state intelligence agency in a country you're working with, but most effectively you can turn to the underworld."

- Barsamian, David. <u>An interview with Alfred McCoy</u>; University of Wisconsin-Madison. Feb 17, 1990

I invite you to take the opportunity to re-read that quote if you feel the need to - if you think you somehow misunderstood that passage, or if there was something that just didn't quite make sense. But I assure you, it's no less difficult to digest a second time around. If you are honest with yourself, and can look realistically and objectively at the history of the actions taken by this country, then you won't need to re-read anything.

Pause... Digest...

The film "What Black Men Think"(2007), produced and directed by Janks Morton, makes the claim that the Black Civil Rights Movement was thrown off course by the Mainstream Civil Rights Movement, which started around 1965 and lasted into the early 70's. It makes the assertion that the shift in collective consciousness from "We" to "*Me*", virtually ruined Black America. And I would add that more so than the Mainstream Civil Rights Movement of war protests, women's rights, and college campus unrest, the Vietnam War itself significantly diverted the country's attention away from the plight of African-Americans. Feeling powerless and helpless at the same time, in light of shady politics and the impending doom of a slanted military draft, the majority of young Americans spiraled into a freefall of escapism; attempting to flee from the overwhelming yet inescapable realities of the time.

Here's something to consider, in the mid 1960's, before the draft, before Vietnam, and before Heroin, 80% of African-American households were 2 parent households. I find this extremely interesting given the current state of the average African-American household, especially in light of the following passage I stumbled across while searching the Internet for information pertaining to the welfare system. The excerpt comes from the Welfare System section of the U.S. History Encyclopedia on the website www.answers.com:

In 1960, the Aid to Families with Dependent Children (AFDC) program cost less than $1 billion and reached 745,000 families. By 1971, it cost $6 billion and reached over 3 million families. The expansion of AFDC was due in part to the concentration of poverty among certain demographic groups, such as African Americans and women. Due to the mechanization of southern agriculture, many African Americans moved northward into urban areas where the unemployment rate was high because of a decrease in factory jobs. The "feminization of poverty" left many women in economic need due to an increasing divorce rate, increasing out-of-wedlock births, and increasing rates of child desertion by fathers.

Although social security remained a much larger program than AFDC, AFDC became more controversial. Beginning in the mid-1970s, the expansion of the AFDC program fueled fears of a growing welfare crisis. As inner cities suffered the effects of deindustrialization and high unemployment, poverty increasingly came to be associated with African Americans living in urban centers, who were often referred to in public discourse as an underclass living in a debilitating culture of poverty. The public image of the AFDC recipient increasingly became that of the welfare mom—presumed to be an unwed African American. Here, the stigma of being poor and the stigma of single motherhood were combined to create a potent racial stereotype.

- U.S. History Encyclopedia: Welfare System.

Reliance on the Welfare System, and on the government, was one of the rare instances in history, where the African-American community can honestly say that it inflicted more pain and suffering on itself, than any other outside force or entity. With our community in disarray, and our potential leaders unwilling, unable -or simply and legitimately scared- to step up, we, for the first time since the slavery days, looked to outside forces to help us. We looked to -and depended upon- the same government that had enslaved us, neglected us, and not only allowed but furthered and facilitated the destruction of our communities, to swoop into our lives like some federally funded Robin Hood and fix all of our problems.

Again, the film *What Black Men Think* argues that the phenomenon of the "feminization of poverty" is a condition which came about due to the Welfare system. It argues that because of the financial reward of having no male present in the household, the Welfare system actually served to create a rift in the Black household as young African-American women were more willing to go it alone in the raising of a family. I would add that the presence and impact of drugs in our communities also had a significant role in the "feminization" of poverty. In actuality, our dependence on the government only allowed 'the powers that be' to further force their own agendas down our throats. It gave them more ammunition for their war on the Black community, on the Black family, the Black male, and on the African-American psyche as a whole!

I also find it interesting that not once does the Answers.com excerpt mention the impact of the Vietnam War on either mainstream American society, or its impact upon the *"certain demographic groups, such as African Americans and women,"* in which there was a *"concentration of poverty"*. The Vietnam War seriously and adversely affected the African-American, minority, and poor White communities of America, as those were the communities most likely, percentage-wise, to be effected by the draft; to have their men shipped off to Southeast Asia. Those were the communities most likely to have their men die in combat, infected with chemicals on the battlefield, or have their men become dependent upon the narcotics found in the Vietnamese jungles. According to information provided by The American War Library:

Of all enlisted men who died in Vietnam, (African-Americans) made up 14.1% of the total. This came at a time when they made up 11% of the young male population nationwide... Of the 7,262

(African-Americans) who died, 6,955, or 96% were Army and Marine enlisted men. .. Early in the war, when (African-Americans) made up about 11% of (the) Vietnam force, (African-American) casualties soared to over 20% of the total (1965-1966).

- The American War Library. Figures obtained from the Vietnam War Memorial; accessed July 17, 2008

Drafted African-American soldiers were un-proportionately the most likely to be assigned to the Army and Marine Corps branches of the U.S. Military; both branches being the first to go to battle, and the most likely to suffer casualties. The governments' identification of Hispanic/Latino individuals during this time period in American history is so archaic that it is very difficult to ascertain the War's impact on those communities; and quite frankly a lot of those identification issues still persist. But even still, according to The American War Library, White and African-American deaths accounted for 98.6% of all American casualties in Vietnam.

The war did much more than leave tens of thousands of American soldiers and Vietnamese peoples dead, maimed, and addicted. It did much more than destroy a country, while leaving another dazed, confused, and divided. It killed the momentum of a much needed movement, at a critical point in its development. More than any of that, the war presented the perfect opportunity for the American government to unleash a new and devastating weapon upon the African-American community; while simultaneously furthering its quest to spread American global influence. That weapon has gone by many handles and nicknames, all too cute to truly intimate the substance's impact, so for the purposes of this text we shall refer to it by its proper name: Heroin. As Professor McCoy explains:

"When the Americans moved into Indochina after the French departed in 1955, we picked up the same tribes, the Hmong, the same politics of narcotics, the politics of heroin, that the French had established. By the 1960's we were operating, particularly the CIA, in collusion with the major traffickers exporting from the mountains not only to meet the consumption needs of Southeast Asia itself, but (also) America's combat forces fighting in Vietnam and ultimately the world market. Southeast Asia today is the number one source of American heroin. That's our major source."

- Barsamian, David. <u>An interview with Alfred McCoy</u>; University of Wisconsin-Madison. Feb 17, 1990

When questioned about the apparent or at least assumed conflict of interest in funding a war through such means, but also introducing American soldiers - and in a broader scope American society - to Heroin, McCoy goes on to explain the general thought process of the country's power structure at that time.

"The CIA had two problems - or the American ruling class - whoever these invisibles are that control this complex uncontrollable country – supposedly had two problems. One was insurgency of minorities. I'm speaking of black uprisings in the cities of America. Another was winning the war in Vietnam. So they put one and one together and they came up with two: the Southeast Asian drug trade...*Potentially insurgent youth has been narcoticized. Write him off for black power.*"

The last line of that quote is bolded for a reason. That line is the reason for this book! That line is the result, the reality, and the backdrop for much of our media programming of today! To apply it more broadly all that is needed are minor adjustments. *Potentially insurgent* can be replaced with potentially politically active, potentially educated, potentially productive, etc. Write him off *for black power* can be replaced with write him off for college, write him off for gainful employment, write him off for political involvement, write him off for society. Write him off period.

This is the phenomenon we must guard against. These are the results we must change. This is the situation which is of the utmost importance within our community. And if we don't address these issues quickly, well - they say that if you do not know your history, then you are doomed to repeat it.

Chapter 5

The Hazy 70's

The end of the Vietnam War not only meant the cessation of an ultimately senseless and devastating military engagement; a furious and deadly ideological debate between communism and democracy. It not only meant the long awaited and for the most part welcomed (*Remember, in times of war a few old men make decisions, and many young men die because of them; those who chastised our entire military corps were foolish and misguided) return of our young American soldiers. It also meant the return of several thousand Heroin addicts as it is estimated that nearly half (50%) of the soldiers in Vietnam were introduced to the narcotic. It brought about a shift in the recreational drug-use scene of mainstream America.

Although naively innocent, what had started out as a mind-expanding, socially bonding, artistically elevating experiment with LSD and marijuana – with people such as Harvard Professor Timothy Leary leading the psychedelic charge - quickly turned into a national crisis with the injection of heroin into the veins of American society. There is a saying that everything is fine in moderation, but if young America was simply testing the waters of drug use in the 1960's, then it seems as though there was a collective decision to dive right in during the 1970's.

It is at this point in the country's history where things really begin to get interesting to me, in terms of the role that the government plays in the lives of the American people – in particular the poor and the urban - because it is at this point when you begin to see a decidedly divisive and destructive approach to dealing with those communities. While the country was indeed facing a major drug-use epidemic, the manner in which those in power decided to deal with it was much more than questionable; some would deem it criminal.

In 1972 President Richard Nixon waged a politically savvy 'War on Drugs'. In reality, little more than a media friendly public relations stunt, Nixon's war actually worsened the country's drug problem as it cut-off only a single and minor avenue of Heroin importation, while opening the floodgates to virtually everything else. The administrations' imaginative manipulation of addiction, death, and crime-rate statistics, coupled with skewed socioeconomic representation in the media, served to create a significant amount of public outcry for something to be done. And in 1973 the American public was introduced to the United States Drug Enforcement Agency (the D.E.A.).

I find it ironic, although completely understandable, that the government would go to such lengths to quash a predicament they themselves engineered. But it's less of a puzzle to me when I look at the situation in terms of an experiment which got out of hand, almost like a runaway train, or the Frankenstein monster – a collection of parts which developed its own consciousness, independent of the inventors' intentions. In reality, the only crisis in the eyes of the government wasn't the fact that there were illegal drugs flowing into the streets of America, but that they had somehow *lost control of that flow.*

It has always been a conspiracy theory of mine that after the assassinations of Malcolm X, and Dr. King – after the SNCC and

Black Panther Party had been successfully stifled and stymied - someone in the government and someone in the entertainment industry - or maybe even a rouge group of individuals with their hands in both arenas - got together and decided that since the African-American community no longer had the leadership of the aforementioned duo (Malcolm and Martin), now (the 70's) would be the perfect time to highlight and glorify everything self-destructive in the 'Black' community, in the hopes that these examples would be accepted by the community -especially the youth- as the next best viable options for success. And after considering everything that we've covered so far, that thought has become exceedingly less conspiracy and substantially more theory.

Marketing Terms:

Guerrilla marketing is an unconventional way of performing promotional activities on a very low budget. Such promotions are sometimes *designed so that the target audience is left unaware they have been marketed to* and may therefore be a form of undercover marketing (also called stealth marketing).

Viral marketing is a marketing phenomenon that facilitates and encourages people to *pass along a marketing message voluntarily*.

Astroturfing is a term for formal public relations campaigns in politics and advertising that seek to create the impression of being spontaneous, grassroots behavior. The goal of such a campaign is to *disguise the agenda of a client as an independent* *public reaction* to some political entity—a politician, political group, product, service or event.

Maybe you've heard of these films?

Shaft (Metro-Goldwyn Meyer / Warner Bros) 1971

Actor Richard Roundtree plays "Shaft", a New York City based, smooth African-American private eye who gets manipulated and forced into a battle between a Black Crime mob, local Black Nationalists, and the Mafia.

Cleopatra Jones (Warner Bros) 1973

Tamara Dobson stars as Cleopatra Jones, a female 007 of sorts, who travels the world confronting drug pushers. This film focuses on Cleopatra's attempts to thwart Mommy, a lesbian drug kingpin, played by Shelly Winters.

Black Caesar (American International Pictures) 1973

Drugs. Crime. Violence. The mafia, and an aspiring young black criminal kingpin. Need I say more.

The Mack (New Line Cinema) 1973

One of the most successful Blackspoitation films of its time, The Mack dealt with the quasi autobiographical story of Max Jullien, a Bay Area pimp. Some of the more famous and infamous themes and images of the entire genre, like The Players Ball, for example, are found in this film.

Dolomite (Dimension Pictures) 1975

Comedian and actor Rudy Ray Moore plays Dolemite, a club owner and pimp, who is set-up by his arch-enemy and sent to prison. A madam by the name of Queen Bee (Lady Reed) arranges for Dolemite to be released, and Dolemite and his army of kung-fu trained prostitutes hit the streets for revenge.

Mandingo (Paramount Pictures) 1975

Ken Norton stars as "Mede", the prize-fighting Mandingo slave, in this film. Mede is not only the most physically imposing slave on the plantation, but also the object of lust and desire for his master's white wife.

Boss Nigger (Dimension Pictures) 1975

 Two Black bounty hunters become sheriff's in a corrupt western town.

Are you beginning to see a pattern; the glorification of drugs, pimping, or crime perhaps? The repetitive and glorified images of violent, street smart, ruthless young black men and women, maybe? And to be sure, these are just a few of the titles from the blackspoitation era. There were many, many more films made with similar plots, similar characters, and similar outcomes.

Now I ask you, do you honestly believe that had Martin and Malcolm survived the 1960's, had they not been struck down by assassins bullets, and had their messages had the opportunity to grow and evolve as they themselves grew and evolved, do you honestly think that these films would have been as successful as they were? Had Heroin not ripped apart and devastated the inner-city black family would these films have resonated so strongly within the urban youth psyche? Would they have been met with box-office acclaim, or with protests, marches, and sit-ins? Would they have been celebrated, or would they have been challenged for the negative imagery and messages they contained? Would there have been so many of them made? Would they have been so popular?

I offered the aforementioned marketing terms for a reason. Guerilla marketing, or stealth marketing, is a mechanism of propaganda spreading which cannot be underestimated for the impact it can have upon a target group. Its main strength is its relentlessness; its repetitive nature –seen in the Blackspoitation films through the repeated images and messages of drugs, crime, pimping, etc., as well as the overall volume of the films themselves. Viral marketing is just that; a virus. It is a way of crafting a message so that people readily accept it and willingly pass it along to others. In essence, it's a way of making something seem as though it is 'common sense', or the accepted way of things –like the trumped-up and overstated *realities* of inner-city living for example.

And now the final term, astroturfing, which relates to a public relations technique of falsely supplanting "the agenda of a client as an independent public reaction" can be understood as the notion that Blackspoitation films were actually a celebration of African-American strengths. It is the persuasive technique utilized by proponents of blackspoitation films who make the claim that they somehow provided positive underlying messages of empowerment and equality for the African-American community. They'll look at a film like Shaft and say "Now there's an example of a strong black man taking a stand to clean up his community." They would probably make the case that Cleopatra Jones is a powerful example of the grace, beauty, and majesty of the African-American woman. They might make the case that, "if you just look past all the pimps and the hoes, the story of The Mack is really the story of the American Dream; a rags to riches tale." Well, to all of that I say that I am sorry, but I call it like I see it. I know propaganda when I see it, and what I see in those films in particular, and in most films of the time, is the obvious and divisive exploitation of an entire community at a time when the community itself was most fragile. I see harmful intent and opportunism on the part of those running the Hollywood studios and production companies. And I argue that any positive messages which can be gleaned from any of those films are overshadowed by the overall tone and theme of the entire genre.

One more definition:

Internalization –

1. To make internal, personal, or subjective.
2. *To take in and make an integral part of one's attitudes or beliefs.*

   - American Heritage Dictionary

Repetition is the key to memorization. Repetition of images and ideas is also the key to the internalization of those images and themes. Therefore, one does not need to be a genius to realize that the more you are told and shown that you are dangerous, or ignorant, or that all that you can be is a pimp, prostitute, drug dealer, entertainer or athlete, the more likely it is that you will internalize these ideas and themes into your psyche in terms of how you 'see' yourself; the more likely that this will occur subconsciously, without your even being aware of it. Our media system, especially in today's ultra-accessible instant messenger society, is our country's most influential and pervasive socializer. More than we know, or would even like to admit, it shapes and creates the frame of reference for both child and adult in terms of how we deal with each other as people; how we see ourselves, and how outsiders view us.

Although a concept that has lost favor in most sociology circles, for both its racial and imperialistic undertones, Environmental Determinism is a theory which has - at its roots – some substantial merit. At the heart of Environmental Determinism, as it relates to sociology, is the idea that an individual's or a community's immediate reality - its living space, its social network, its resources, its opportunities, its wealth or lack thereof – are all important indicators as to how successful or productive that individual or community will be. In the American social experiment that is our society, and quite honestly all throughout human history, we have seen examples of this. When those with the most are given the most, and those with the least are given the least, the outcomes of success have been predetermined.

In relation to the nature vs. nurture debate, environmental determinism is most easily depicted in the theme behind the novel *Rich Dad, Poor Dad* by Robert Kiyosaki and Sharon Lechter (Warner Books, 2000). The book itself, a New York Times best-seller, is a novel which details the type of information disseminated in the households of the wealthy as opposed to that offered in the homes of the less fortunate; basically, it's an explanation of the sort of cultural and socioeconomic 'leg-up' given to those who already have a decided advantage in life opportunities. It's a comparison of 'best practices' utilized by those who know as opposed to those who are just guessing.

In terms of the physical reality of environmental determinism, one need only look at the myriad examples offered by virtually all major American cities - and quite honestly, by all major cities in any country – to see first hand the impact of ones surroundings and resources upon their ability to succeed. The "ghetto" is referred to as the ghetto for a reason, "uptown" is known as uptown for a reason. Just like Black and White, they are two ends of the spectrum; they are definers of each other. In the ghetto you have blight, you have poverty, you have desperation. The kinds of social realities those situations produce – especially when combined and compounded over time - are a lack of optimism, a culture of drugs and crime, and a dearth of hope so deep that entire communities can sink into a mind-state of hopelessness.

Add to that the constant and pervasive negative and violent images and messages of an unbalanced and biased media system, and the implications for a community are often catastrophic. That is the main issue that I have with the Blackspoitation film era; an era in which Black images were *celebrated* on the big screen through a long parade of pimps, pushers, and hoes. An era in which one would be hard pressed to find a feature film that did not play heavily upon one or more incredibly harmful stereotypes pertaining to the African-American community. To that end, the mental or thought process implications of environmental determinism can sometimes be the most devastating to a community. Because as young people are constantly shown only the negative aspects of themselves, and when those images and messages are paired with substandard living spaces and resources, the impact on the human spirit can be fatal – not only for the youngster, but for anyone unlucky enough to cross that youngster, because if he doesn't value his own life then you don't need to be a genius to realize how much value he places on yours.

....

The Big Picture

California's Prop 13

- California's Prop 13 was an all out "tax revolt" brought about and supported by predominantly white wealthy and upper-middle class Californians outraged at their ever-increasing property taxes. Lead by a wealthy retired industrialist by the name of Howard Jarvis, and retired real estate magnate Paul Gann, the proposition garnered a landslide political victory in the state even amongst warnings "that schools may not be able to educate, libraries may close and crime rates may climb", according to a 1978 Time magazine article.

- During the same timeframe of the Prop 13 passing, voters in Ohio denied 89 of 139 school tax levies aimed at saving Cleveland and Columbus area public schools.

- Within 5 years, 37 states enacted similar propositions.

- This is a major turning point in the educational standards of America; the defining moment of "have and have not" status –well-funded and barely-funded schooling, or in other words, private versus public schooling.

....

Chapter 6

The 80's – Crack-Cocaine and Gang Violence

On August 18, 1996, San Jose Mercury News journalist Gary Webb broke a story entitled "America's 'crack' plague has roots in Nicaragua war". The story detailed the formation of a CIA backed guerilla force in Nicaragua, which was formed with the intent of overthrowing the socialist government of that country. The story also elaborated on how the guerrillas funded their 'movement' through U.S. government assisted drug smuggling and arms dealing in North American ghettos. Sound familiar? *See Vietnam War, if not.

The story described in detail how the CIA not only formed the Guerilla force in 1981, but also safe-guarded U.S. based Nicaraguan front-men for the Guerrilla force from prosecution by local and government authorities. These front-men used a young African-American contact by the name of Ricky Donnel Ross, or "Freeway Rick" as he was known, to funnel guns, ammunition, and drugs to the greater Los Angeles community (most notably South Central L.A.) as a means of financing their 'coup'. These actions would spawn the era of the Bloods and Crips; as the rival gangs began to battle for drug-pushing territory.

"While the Nicaraguan Democratic Force (FDN)'s war is barely a memory today, black America is still dealing with its poisonous side effects. Urban neighborhoods are grappling with legions of homeless crack addicts. Thousands of young black men are serving long prison sentences for selling cocaine – a drug that was virtually unobtainable in black neighborhoods before members of the CIA's army started bringing it into South Central in the 1980s at bargain-basement prices."

- Gary Webb, "America's 'crack' plague has roots in Nicaragua War", 1996

They say that if you do not know your history, you are doomed to repeat it. But here we have a situation where a history, or more succinctly a back-story, has been hidden from the community it affected most, and that community is oblivious to, and therefore unable to recognize the identical mechanisms which are once again put in motion to maintain its suppression. And so the billion dollar question becomes how does one protect himself from following the same destructive pattern if he's not even aware that he was ever in that pattern to begin with? How do you cope with drug addiction in the ghetto if you have no control over drug flow into the ghetto?

With respect to that influx of foreign-grown drugs and military grade munitions finding their way into urban American neighborhoods, there is one man in particular, who truly knows the extent to which said flow was initiated by, monitored by, and orchestrated through American government interests; and that man's name is Oliver North. In 1988 Senator John Kerry led a Senate Foreign Relations subcommittee investigation into accusations of foul play with regards to the funding of Nicaraguan contras; especially in relation to the conflict of the source of that funding with America's War on Drugs. The major player at the center of that investigation was North himself, who was the Reagan Administration's National Security Council aide in charge of the operation of the contra war. The Kerry led committee found that "Mr. North, then on the National Security Council staff at the White House, and other senior officials created a privatized contra network that attracted drug traffickers looking for cover for their operations, then turned a blind eye to repeated reports of drug smuggling related to the contras, and actively worked with known drug smugglers such as Panamanian dictator Manuel Noriega to assist the contras." (The National Security Archive; produced by George Washington University. Peter Kornbluh, Feb 26, 2004)

The FDN war in Nicaragua - which had no correlation to the well-being of American society win or lose, aside from the devastation of drugs and violence felt within America's "expendable" communities - provided the American elite with the same opportunity to incorporate the practice and politics of narcotics that the Vietnam War offered nearly a decade and a half before. It is my belief that the American government - those invisible powers that be – applied pressure to the mainstream American media to create a hostile environment for Gary Webb and his expose. From the L.A. Times to the N.Y. Times, and even the Washington Post, Gary Webb received ridicule and harsh critique from nearly all of his major media colleagues; even after government officials produced evidence supporting Webb's story.

It should however, be noted that Webb's story, along with public outcry from the African-American community, as well as sympathetic white supporters, prompted an earnest Justice Department investigation. Yet even after the investigation produced such damning evidence as the identification of more than 50 contras and contra-related entities implicated in the drug trade, and even after proof of Reagan-Bush administration cover-up had been furnished, and even still after evidence was provided that the drug-trafficking and money laundering could be traced into Reagan's National Security Council - the organization through which Oliver North directed the contra operations - the major American media outlets were virtually mum on the subject.

(Robert Parry, "America's debt to Gary Webb", December 13, 2004) To revisit some of the tactics utilized with the Cointelpro efforts:

"Much of the Bureau's propaganda efforts involved giving information or articles to 'friendly' media sources who could be relied upon not to reveal the Bureau's interests... 156 field offices also had 'confidential sources' (unpaid Bureau informants) in the media, and were able to ensure their cooperation. The Bureau's use of the news media took two different forms: placing unfavorable articles and documentaries about targeted groups, and leaking derogatory information intended to discredit individuals." (Select Committee Final Report; book 3, p.24-25)

It would not be out of the question to envision the Bureau using its influence to keep certain stories out of the mainstream news outlets as well. Now it is important to keep in mind the timeframe of these events. The actual occurrence of the FDN Nicaraguan conflict took place between the early to mid-1980's, however the report of and investigation into these events would not occur until the mid-late 1990's. I find it extremely interesting and not so coincidental that only months after the Justice Departments' investigative report was released in 1998 -two years after Webb's story broke in 1996- the Monica Lewinsky scandal broke loose in the Mainstream American Media and held captive the hearts and minds of the American public.

Smoke and mirrors, I say, smoke and mirrors! And to be quite honest, I wouldn't put it past *the powers that be* in this country (or at least a rogue faction of *them*), to have purposely leaked the Lewinsky scandal at such an opportune time. The Lewinsky scandal was America's first true taste of the captivatingly mind-numbing experience that is reality television.

To the suggestion of 'a rogue faction' acting on behalf of a select group of interests within this country, according to a Wikipedia report, the term Cryptocracy, which derives its root from the ancient Greek words kryptós, meaning *hidden,* and krateín, meaning *to rule*, refers to a type of government where the real leaders are hidden, or unknown. It is the type of system in which a puppet government or figurehead, *whether aware or not of their status as such*, is in apparent but not actual control. (Wikipedia. Cited 11/12/08) Up to and maybe even including the current administration, to certain -although I would hope much lesser- extents, this term would more than likely accurately describe the ruling structure utilized throughout the entirety of this country's history. And it would definitely be an accurate portrayal of the Nixon, Reagan, and Bush Administration (both Sr. and Jr.) years of Washington, in the eyes of many political pundits. In an in depth interview conducted by Uri Dowbenko, government watchdog and CEO of New Improved Entertainment Corp., with retired U.S. Naval Intelligence officer Al Martin, Martin defines a cryptocracy as a "government within a government, comprising of some thirty to forty thousand people the American government turns to, when it wishes certain illegal covert operations to be extant pursuant to a political objective."

So if this is the case, and you have a situation in which the whistle has been blown concerning the type of corruption which includes weapons and drug trafficking o.k.'d by those in the highest offices and levels of government, what type of actions do you think a so-called cryptocracy might take? Creating a sensational -although by no means novel- news story to capture and distract the nation's attention might be one. The removal of the trouble-makers and whistle blowers altogether might be another.

There is an age old adage that states that, 'When you speak the truth to power you run a risk.' His ground breaking and eye-opening expose would cost Gary Webb his life; both figuratively, as his career and marriage would begin to unravel as external pressures proved to strong for either to survive, and literally, as on Friday, Dec. 10, 2004, Gary Webb, at age 49, was found dead in his apartment of an *apparent suicide*, with a gunshot wound to the head. On December 13, 2004, fellow journalist and friend of Webb, Robert Parry, wrote a story entitled "America's Debt to Journalist Gary Webb". Parry, who has also covered many of the Iran-Contra stories of the 1980s, used recently declassified government documents, and court testimonials to make the claim that Webb had only touched the tip of the iceberg of the CIA-backed drug and arms smuggling operation:

"According to evidence cited by the report, the Reagan-Bush administration knew almost from the outset of the contra war that cocaine traffickers permeated the paramilitary operation. The administration also did next to nothing to expose or stop the criminal activities. The report revealed example after example of leads not followed, corroborated witnesses disparaged, official law-enforcement investigations sabotaged, and even the CIA facilitating the work of drug traffickers."

"The (Justice Department Inspector General) Michael Bromwich report showed that the contras and their supporters ran several parallel drug-smuggling operations, not just the one at the center of Webb's series. The report also found that the CIA shared little of its information about contra drugs with law-enforcement agencies and on three occasions disrupted cocaine-trafficking investigations that threatened the contras."

- Robert Parry, "America's debt to Gary Webb", December 13, 2004

And while the FBI and CIA were definitely major players in many of the covert and illegal actions taken on behalf of certain American interests, in the previously mentioned interview with Dowbenko, Al Martin asserts that the real force behind the country's covert actions -the agency which lends its influence to ensure the credibility and success of said actions- is the Office of Naval Intelligence (or ONI). According to Martin, as where the public personas of politicians and their traceable links to individuals within the CIA and FBI can be limiting or compromising to those agencies with respect to certain endeavors, the beauty of ONI is that it is able to operate in a relatively unknown, but very out-in-the-open manner. As Martin states:

"The principals (i.e., main players) of the ONI faction are people that you wouldn't know…Their power comes from the fact that they're not known. Their names wouldn't really mean anything, therefore they can act in such a behind-the-scenes fashion- much more than the CIA… They're very deep in old contacts… They are able to blend overt and covert operations in the same breath because they are essentially not a covert agency like the CIA. It allows them great cover to operate in the open."

In a more global sense, I believe Mr. Martin's assessment to hold some truth, especially in the allowance or conveyance of illegal products or goods to be imported or exported into or out of the country. But with respect to domestic meddling and tampering with the lives of American citizens, I personally give more credit and therefore more blame to the FBI and CIA.

In another Dowbenko article entitled, <u>Dirty Secret: Drug Czar Walters and the Iran Contra Connection</u>, the author details the shady connections of the most recent Bush Administration Drug Czar, John P. Walters. In the article Dowbenko uncovers the bloodlines which connect Walters to the Iran-Contra arms and drug smuggling controversies of the 70's and 80's. According to Dowbenko, "the father of John Walters is US Army Lieutenant General Vernon A. Walters, the deputy director of the CIA from 1972 to 1976 during the Nixon Administration." Vernon Walters was the head of the CIA during the Watergate scandal. And when the former Assistant Secretary of State Elliott Abrams traveled to Panama to convene with Noriega, one of the individuals that accompanied Abrams was the special advisor to the State Department's Office of Inter-American Affairs; none other than John P. Walters. As Dowbenko states:

"Financing the federal deficit and keeping the stock market buoyed actually depends on the daily reinvestment of laundered monies. A large percentage of that depends on the cash flow from the high margin profits of narcotics trafficking, government contract fraud, the burgeoning for-profit prison industry and its concomitant slave labor market- all key components of the phony War on Drugs."

"With his 'hands-on' experience in Iran-Contra drug trafficking, the appointment of John Walters as George Bush's new "drug czar" is a fitting crown for a man who knows what it takes to keep the flow of drugs moving into the country – and the necessary cash flow moving through Wall Street."

- Dowbenko, Uri. Dirty Secret: Drug Czar Walters and the Iran-Contra Connection: Conspiracy Digest. 2001

As the fictitious CIA director Ezra Crammer, played by actor Scott Glenn, in the wildly successful Robert Ludlum based Bourne movie trilogy states, "You can't make this stuff up."

It is during this decade of increased violence and drug-use –
albeit orchestrated by outside players- within the African-
American community, and more so towards the mid to latter-half
of the decade, that the mainstream media does all it can to
bombard the rest of American society with images of 'violent' and
'dangerous' black youths. News report after news report flood
television and radio airwaves regarding the increase in drug use
and drug violence within urban communities, yet no one seems to
be questioning how these drugs and these guns are making their
way into communities which have no way of producing either of
them.

When looking at the not so coincidental connection between
Hollywood and real life, I find it to be no mere matter of
happenstance that one of the most popular gangster movies of all
time, *Scarface* (Universal Pictures), is released in 1983; adding to
the 'glory' and allure of drug trafficking in ghettos all throughout
the country.

Ah, Scarface, now there's a cultural phenomenon if ever
there was one. And not a phenomenon designated to any specific
culture, ethnically speaking at least, even though it centered on a
specific Latin American experience in this country. Scarface is
without question the most popular gangster / drug related movie of
all time. It is the story of Cuban immigrant Tony Montana - played
by a young Al Pacino - a rags to riches story steeped in drugs,
money laundering and murder; the ultimate get rich or die trying
storyline, and as some have characterized it, the ultimate American
Dream story. As a movie, it is without question entertaining, but
what is extremely interesting to me is that for countless young men
and women in this country, especially those living in slum-like
conditions similar to Montana, Scarface the movie became
Scarface the blueprint for "success"; Scarface the dogma. As
rapper Jay-Z states, "Scarface the actor did more than Scarface the
rapper to me." The movie captured the hearts and minds of almost

any young person living in poverty as they mentally placed themselves in Montana's shoes and pondered the possibilities – "Wouldn't that be nice?" It's one of the reasons that nearly every rapper, entertainer, or athlete of color will make mention of the movie during their segment of Mtv's hit show Cribs.

Here again, Scarface the movie is a prime example of the media's glorification of the quick-fix; the instant gratification of fast, dangerous money, and all the trappings that come along with it. It doesn't even seem to matter to most that Scarface's main character, Tony Montana, meets an untimely and brutal demise at the hands of a Columbian hit squad; especially given the fact that even his death is presented in a symbolic, if not heroic way, as if to say that that's how a man should go out – with guns a blazin'- *"Say hello to my little friend!"* This is the main issue I take with the image of 50 Cent, it's the same issue I take with the Godfather movies, most movies depicting ghetto life, and more recently the film and BET channel series of the same name -which chronicles the stories of fabled ghetto criminals- American Gangster. How many times must we watch the same movies, with the same themes, with the same outcomes? They add nothing to the conversation of advancement or change, nor do they speak to conditions of which society is not aware. They do, however, contribute greatly to the allure of crime. And I am quite simply dumbfounded by the decision of the Black Entertainment Television (BET) network to air a series such as the American Gangster chronicles. Really?!? Is that what our community needs? Is that what our young people should be watching; a gangster do-it-yourself television series?

Sometimes I just wish that those of us who are in the position to really affect some change within our community, the Robert Johnsons and Sean "P. Diddy" Combs of the African-American community -those of us in control of at least some of the messages that are geared towards us – would ask themselves this simple question, "Would Malcolm or Martin approve of this?" That's really a question most of our entertainers need to be asking themselves. Profit-margin aside, is this going to help or harm my community?

The late 1970's and early 80's ushered in a new era in American media standards and advertising. In the more general mainstream American society, blatant racism and bigotry were taking a turn toward the unfashionable. Oh the sentiments still existed, but their outright public expressions were no longer acceptable in most American communities; or at least ones with significant minority populations - which at that point in time now accounted for all types of Latin and Hispanic peoples, Pacific Islander, Korean, Vietnamese, and Filipino peoples - due in large part to the passing of the Immigration Act of 1965. The constant influx of more and more non-white peoples had forced white America to at least act civil within the confines of public discourse. In response to this growing contingent of minorities in American cities and suburban communities, American businesses and the media began to focus attention to the *spending power* of its new citizens; and so for the first time we begin to see multicultural advertising and programming.

While Doctor J may have been the first major American athlete endorsed by a shoe company when Converse inked the high flying star to a shoe deal in 1976, it would be Michael Jordan and his ground breaking 5 year, 2.5 million dollar shoe deal with Nike in 1984, that would change the face of the athletic endorsement world. As is reported on Sneakerhead.com, the website dedicated to all knowledge shoe apparel related, the Air Jordan shoe deal was ground-breaking and controversial. As the site reports, "(due to the color styling) The NBA banned the shoe from the league, but Jordan wore them anyway, racking up serious fines of up to $5,000 a game. Nike, of course, was more than happy to pay (the fines) to keep the shoes on Jordan's feet and in the public eye. All this controversy and Jordan's spectacular numbers that year served to put the Air Jordan line on the road to becoming a household name." And that's exactly what happened. Jordan became an international phenomenon, and the Nike brand soared in sales and in prominence.

Although they were no doubt the most popular, Air Jordan's weren't the only shoes on the block. With the explosion of Hip-Hop in the mid 1980's, the African-American influence on young urban fashion would take hold with the help of songs like Run DMC's "My Adidas". Sweatsuits, Kangol hats, and Ray Bans would become the fashion statement of the decade behind LL Cool J's popularity as a young brash rapper. What was beginning to take shape all across America, from the ghettos to the suburbs, was what would come to be known as the Namebrand Phenomenon; the ultimate fashion arms race! In order to be considered cool, hip, or down, you couldn't wear just any pair of shoes, you had to wear a specific brand of shoes, a specific brand of sweatsuit, a specific brand of sunglasses, etc. And in the suburbs, the explosion of Rock and Roll and Heavy Metal music, thanks in part to Mtv, would lead itself to other fashion trends. The 80's were a fun time of fashionable athletic wear, gaudy jewelry, and exaggerated accessories in the urban areas of the country, along with big hair, stonewashed jeans, and vibrant bright colors in the suburbs. And in the beginning, as is the case with most things, it was all innocent enough.

I'm not quite sure exactly when it happened, but somewhere along the way, once the corporate and media giants realized what they had, things began to take a turn towards the outrageous. Once

Air Jordan's and Nike became household names, and once it became known that the shoe that Michael Jordan wore was the shoe of choice for every little brown boy and girl in America's city streets and suburban playgrounds, the decision makers at Nike decided to jack the prices of their product sky-high (to resemble their stock shares perhaps).

A sound business decision no doubt: simple supply and demand economics. There aren't too many Wall Street veterans that would find fault with the ways in which Nike, Adidas, and Reebok conducted their business operations in those days. The vibrancy and success of those companies during those times reflects everything inherent in the American economic philosophy of capitalism. The issue I have is that once these companies had successfully captured the interest and brand loyalty of the urban market upon which they had lavished so much attention and efforts, they began to out-price their core market – leading to violence on inner-city streets as youth began to kill for fashion sake; a reality not mourned but secretly celebrated by sneaker executives. "We've got something special here boys. They're willing to kill for these things!" The quote-un-quote Sneaker Wars between Nike and Reebok, morphed into actual street violence as young, impressionable, and extremely poor youths were willing to risk any and everything in an effort to achieve the street status that a pair of the *flyest* kicks guaranteed. As if the escalating price of Air Jordan sneakers had not been enough, I recall that the day news broke about a young black boy being murdered for his sneakers, my dad made the decision to stop buying them all together. We didn't own another pair of Nike shoes for some time after that.

The 1980's are a tremendously interesting and incredibly important time period in the development of the African-American community; especially in terms of our presence in the media. Our athletes were reaching unprecedented levels of notoriety, not only nationally, but internationally as well. The emergence of Hip-Hop as a musical genre would have an unforeseeable and ever evolving impact upon the community. Towards the middle of the decade, for the first time, we would begin to see some truly positive and uplifting African-American representation on daytime and prime-time television.

The Cosby Show is probably the single-most uplifting example that I can offer. After viewing his Tonight Show monologue on child rearing, NBC executives recruited actor, comedian, and current social commentator Bill Cosby, to create one of the most unique, positive, and inspiring African-American family oriented sitcoms this country, ergo the world, had or has ever seen. The show focused on the lives of Dr. Clifford Huxtable (played by Bill Cosby), his wife, lawyer Claire Huxtable (played by Felicia Rashad), and their five children. The Huxtables were an upper-middle class African-American family living in Harlem. As Darnell M Hunt reports for the Museum of Broadcast Communications, "Alvin Poussaint, a prominent Black psychiatrist, was hired by producers as a consultant to help "recode blackness" in the minds of audience members... The Huxtables were given a particular mix of qualities that its creators thought would challenge common black stereotypes. These qualities included: a strong father figure, a strong nuclear family, parents who were professionals, affluence and fiscal responsibility, a strong emphasis on education, a multigenerational family, multiracial friends, and low-key racial pride." (www.museum.tv; sited Nov. 2008) The show was wildly popular and incredibly successful, claiming the number one slot in the ratings for 5 straight seasons. Critics main argument was that the show was a little too positive, and that it therefore created an unrealistic picture of the realities facing African-American families. Unlike the shows of its time such as Sanford and Son, Good Times, and The Jeffersons, The Cosby Show rarely dealt with the constant struggle for respect and equality found within the African-American community. And to all of that I say, thank goodness! We cannot always be bogged down by grim images and daunting statistics. When you are fully aware of your reality, you do not *always* need to be reminded of it. Sometimes we need to be able to dream; to aspire to greater heights and greener pastures. Sometimes, we need the Cosbys.

The Cosby show would have its own similarly successful spin-off entitled A Different World, which was a series chronicling the college years of the Huxtables' second eldest daughter Denise. Hillman College was the fictional Historically Black College that Denise attended, and Hillman itself was loosely fashioned after Atlanta's Spellman College. A Different World was tremendously popular and incredibly positive. For me personally, the shows' lead male character Dwayne Wayne, played by Kadeem Hardison, was my first example of what a college educated Black man could be. Dwayne Wayne was the personification of the potential I saw in myself; smart, cool, witty, and seemingly knowledgeable in a vast array of topics. I wanted to someday be like Dwayne Wayne. I even searched high and low for his trademark double-pained flip-up sunglasses. That character was an incredibly positive impact upon my young and impressionable self. The show itself was an incredibly positive impact upon all young African-American children. Because of the age demographic of the show's main characters, the series was able to touch upon a wider and more mature array of topics than the very family oriented Cosby Show. Everything from teenage dating to race issues was touched upon during the show's tenure, and we watched as the young freshman of Hillman grew into young successful adults, ready to take on the world.

In 1984, an extremely talented and ambitious young woman by the name of Oprah Winfrey would become the first African-American host of a daytime television talk show. Although her ascension to the heights of the media world had begun several years before, seemingly overnight Oprah had captured the hearts and minds of America's stay at home moms and revolutionized daytime television, beginning her journey towards becoming one of the most successful TV personalities of all time -as well as the first, and so far only, African-American female billionaire. The Oprah Winfrey Show was the number one rated talk show for 22 consecutive seasons according the Nielsen rankings report! In 1988, as the head of Harpo Studios, Oprah became only the third woman in American history to own her own television production studio, and in 2008 Oprah and Discovery Communications announced plans to launch OWN: The Oprah Winfrey Network. (Orpah.com; cited Nov. 2008) Today, Oprah has reached Icon status; she is among the likes of Madonna and Bono, Michael Jordan, and Tiger Woods.

A few years down the line, another African-American family sitcom would come along by the name of Family Matters. The show was centered on the daily trials and tribulations of the Winslow family, a comfortable middle-class Chicago family. The star of the show however, would be the Winslow's meddlesome neighbor, and American's all-time favorite geek, Steven Q. Urkell, played by the young and talented actor Jaleel White. With his signature catch phrase "Did I do that?", Urkell would become an overnight sensation, and for the first time in the mainstream media there was a young African-American male that went against all young African –American male stereotypes. He was highly intelligent, socially awkward, and he wouldn't know what to do with a gun if he saw one. He was the antitype to the prototypical mainstream media African-American male, and his presence was both sorely needed and deeply appreciated.

....

The Subtle Tactics of Urban Marketing

In a presentation produced by the Greenfield Consulting Group -a leader in qualitative marketing research- entitled "Understanding the Urban Consumer", and presented to the Advertising Research Foundation, Urban (culture) is defined thusly:

(Urban) Is the intersection of a 'metropolitan mindset' with 'ethnic' young culture. It is a 'gumbo' of several cultural elements including – 'keeping it real', street smarts, fast city living, racial and economic diversity, fusion of ethnic cultures, grass roots sensibilities, and the aesthetics of music subcultutres; namely 'hip-hop'.

The report states that Urban culture influences the mainstream culture in a sequential way; urban youth are innovators and trendsetters which organizations and companies look to in order to adopt and commercialize the trends in an effort to re-package and re-present to the (other) mainstream youth, which in turn become consumers of everything associated with that trend.

The report dissects the urban market demographically, behaviorally, and attitudinally; stating at one point that there is a prevalent *"hustler mentality"* amongst urban youth, although the producers of the report are quick to note that 'hustler' is meant positively.

'Cultural Winks', are advertising methods which intimate a deep and benign understanding of a given culture. According to Greenfield, a 'wink' is defined as:

1) a mainstream ad; in other words, it's not in the 'ethnic' media
2) it's subtle; it doesn't hit you over the head
3) it's devoid of stereotypes
4) it challenges preconceptions
5) it has an insider reference that an outsider would miss
6) it appeals to a mainstream audience, hitting the target consumers sweet spot
7) it elicits a 'That was for us!" response from multicultural viewers.

The instantly famous, Budweiser "Waassssup?!" Super Bowl adds are a perfect example of a cultural wink in advertising.

....

In 1980, a Mississippi born, University of Illinois and Princeton educated African-American man by the name of Bob Johnson, took a $15,000 loan coupled with a $500,000 investment from then CEO of Tele-Communications Inc., John Malone, and founded the television channel known as Black Entertainment Television, or BET. The first television network of its kind, BET's programming catered to the social and leisurely aspects of African-American life. In the early 1980's, with the birth of the Music Television Channel in 1981 -otherwise known as Mtv- the social and leisurely aspects African-American life, as well as those of mainstream American daily life, were most readily and accessibly chronicled in the form of music videos.

Now, it is important to remember that African-American music has always been a reflection of the African-American social situation; be it Jazz, Soul, Hip-Hop, or R&B. Towards the mid to late 1980's, in response to the increasingly harsh realities of urban African-American life, "Gangster Rap" is born. What started with *Niggaz With Attitude* (N.W.A.), quickly morphed into the individual successes of Easy E, MC Ren, Ice Cube, and Doctor Dre, paving the way for the birth of Death Row Records and Snoop Doggy Dogg. Taking the lead from their musical contemporaries on the east coast such as KRS-One and Public Enemy -socially conscious rappers whose rhymes reflected the situations from which they came- West Coast rappers decided it was time America heard their tales from the hood. Never before had such gritty and grimy stories of drive-by-shootings, drug related violence, and gang affiliation been laid out for all to see. The brutal and detailed realities of ghetto violence shocked mainstream America, and at first the media vilified Gangsta Rap. The anger and the venom with which these young men spat their lyrics frightened White America, and emboldened urban and inner-city youths. Finally, someone was saying exactly what they wished they were able to scream –to anyone within listening range.

Young black men quickly shot to the top of the rankings of American's Most Dangerous list; not that they had ever strayed far from the top position. Politicians did everything they could to have the entire musical genre outlawed. The most notable example of which was the reaction to rapper Ice T's song entitled "Cop Killer", which was actually a Rock and Roll song that Ice-T created with his Punk Rock band *Body Count*. But because Ice-T was a young African-American male, "Cop Killer" was classified as Gangsta Rap. What the media, and more widely mainstream America, didn't realize was that their constant and dedicated vilifying of young African-American males only made the plight of young African-American males that much more interesting to young suburban White kids. You have to remember that in most cases, when a rapper or a young black musician goes platinum, it's most likely not because a million African-American children purchased their record. It is my contention that during this time period, the powers that be in America, realized that they could not only make *a lot* of money packaging and selling the 'Gangsta' mentality, but that they could also give a new generation of young African-Americans a new, more violent role model.

....

The Big Picture

Tiananmen Square

- On the 4th of June, 1989, the Chinese Army, at the command of the Chinese government, murdered hundreds –possibly thousands- of Chinese protestors supporting a cause of democratic reform.
- The protestors were mainly students, and the violent eruption was the culmination of several weeks worth of demonstration, which the government considered civil unrest.
- The event is widely regarded as the most significant demonstration against Communism in China's history
- The image most readily associated with this event, and blazoned into the memories of the world's citizens, is that of a single Chinese man, standing in front of a succession of Chinese Army tanks; defiant and triumphant.

HIV/AIDS – Source: The Center for Disease Control

- HIV stands for human immunodeficiency virus; it is the virus that causes AIDS. AIDS stands for acquired immunodeficiency syndrome, and is the final stage of HIV infection. HIV attacks the immune system by finding and destroying a type of white blood cell (T cells) that the immune system must have to fight disease.
- According to the Center for Disease Control, scientists identified a type of chimpanzee in West

Africa as the source of HIV infection in humans. It is speculated that "the virus most likely jumped to humans when humans hunted these chimpanzees for meat and came into contact with their infected blood." However, the exact origin of the disease is unlikely to ever to be known for certain; a situation which has lead to numerous tales and speculations of its true origin.

- HIV was first identified in the United States in 1981, after a number of gay men began getting sick with what was originally misdiagnosed as a rare type of cancer.
- Early on, the disease took on the negative public association of being linked to homosexuality and drug use, until the very public announcement that star Basketball player Earvin 'Magic' Johnson had contracted the virus through unprotected heterosexual sex, in 1991.
- The CDC currently estimates that about 1 million people in the United States are living with HIV/AIDS, and that about a quarter of them are unaware that they are infected.

....

Chapter 7

The 90's: Silver screen, small screen, and the violent streets in between

A Brief Cinematic Timeline

1991 – Boy'z in the Hood (Columbia Pictures)

The story of three inner-city Los Angeles youths, and the different paths that their lives take. Ice Cube stars as street tough 'Doughboy', and Morris Chestnut plays his star athlete half-brother Ricky Baker.

1991 – New Jack City (Warner Bros)

Wesley Snipes plays ruthless drug dealer Nino Brown. Chris Rock plays a crackhead by the name of "Pookie". New Jack City chronicles Nino's rise to power, and fall from grace.

1992 – Juice (Paramount Pictures)

Tupac Shakur and Omar Epps headline this crime drama about a group of four Harlem friends who "spend their days skipping school, getting in fights, and casually shoplifting". Only one of the friends has plans for his future, but those plans are put on hold when a robbery goes wrong.

1992- American Me (Universal Pictures)

A depiction of a generation worth of Chicano gang life in Los Angeles. American Me stars Edward James Olmos as Santana, a young gang member sent to prison for 18 years. While in prison, Santana becomes leader of the Mexican Mafia and rules the ruthless gang from behind bars.

1993 – Menace to Society (New Line Cinema)

An "urban crime drama" set in the Watts neighborhood of Los Angeles, CA. The film focuses on Caine (Tyrin Turner), an 18 year old drug dealer, his friend O-Dog, a vicious street thug, and Caine's girlfriend Ronnie, played by Jada Pinkett Smith.

1993- Strapped (HBO: Osiris Films)

Set in the Brooklyn projects, this film follows a young African-American ex-con attempting to leave his criminal past behind him, but of course this can't happen without first getting into a bit more trouble.

1993 – Carlito's Way (Universal Pictures)

Carlito Brigante, played by Al Pacino, is an ex-con trying to go straight, but of course, his social circle does not allow for that, and just as it seems he is about to escape his sordid past, it all catches up to him.

1993- Blood In Blood Out (Hollywood Pictures)

Based on the true life experiences of poet Jimmy Santiago Baca, the film focuses on half-brothers Paco and Cruz, and their bi-racial cousin Miklo. It opens in 1972, as the three are members of an East L.A. gang known as the "Vatos Locos", and the story focuses on how a violent crime and the influence of narcotics alter their lives.

1994 – Fresh (Paramount Pictures)

The story of a 12 year old inner-city youth by the name of Michael, or Fresh as he's well known throughout his projects, played by actor Sean Nelson. Fresh is a drug runner living in a crowded house with his cousins and aunt. His father is a bum and his sister is a junkie. Sean must use his street smarts and the strategies of chess he's learned from his father, to cheat death and survive the dope game.

1995 - New Jersey Drive (Universal Pictures)

A story of two young black car thieves in Newark, New Jersey – the unofficial car theft capital of the world.

1995 – Mi Familia (New Line Cinema)

A story tracing three generations of a Mexican immigrant family living in East Los Angeles.

1997 – I'm Bout It (No Limit Films)

Rapper Master P, co-wrote and stars in this low budget, cult classic about his experiences as a young New Orleans drug dealer, and his attempts to go straight.

1998 – Colors (Orion Pictures)

A confident young cop is shown the ropes by a veteran partner in the dangerous gang-controlled barrios of L.A., which are about to explode in violence, in this look at the gang culture enforced and informed by the colors that members wear.

So, in the 1990's alone, we have a situation where more than 10 major motion pictures depicting African-American and Hispanic/Latino youth involved in gangs, violence, prison, and drug trafficking, are released in America. And while we know that Hollywood as an industry is about as original as a P.Diddy single, in all honesty, did we really need this many films covering virtually the same material? What new or poignant information did these films add to the American conversation? What new insight did they offer American society as to the major issues affecting urban communities, and more than that, what solutions did they offer to solve those problems?

More to the point, one has to ask himself, were these movies ever really crafted to solve those issues and force those tough questions, or were they merely an effort to glamorize and glorify specific themes to targeted and specific communities. Was this a new era of Blackspoitation films; adapted of course to account for the growing Latino population? And now the 90's were the time period of my childhood. This was the timeframe in American history that I most readily identify with and remember as the apex of my pre-pubescent self. Spending most of my youth in Pomona, California, I remember how fascinated my social group was with movies like Boy'z In the Hood, Juice, Menace to Society, American Me, Blood In Blood Out, I'm Bout it, etc. These were the things we talked about. These were the most readily available and easily accessible silver screen images of people who looked like us, and were supposed to be in our age range, and those were the kinds of things they were doing. Great role models indeed! Quite honestly, had it not been for my solid foundation at home, coupled with my quasi-introvert disposition as a child, I may have gotten caught up in all the hype of *glorified gangsterism* that so many of the children of that time -and today- fell victim to.

Again, the problem is twofold. Those movies may have been geared to, comprised of, and targeted towards urban youth, but that wasn't the only audience their images and messages were disseminated to. The images, messages, and themes of those movies trickled their way out to suburbia and middle-America. They filtered their way into the conversations and concerns of registered voters, politicians, and policy-makers. In short, they scared the hell out of White America.

In conjunction with the manufactured fear machine of Hollywood, were real life struggles and violence within these communities. Oh make no mistake about it, Hollywood didn't need to make these issues up, the violence and crime being depicted in movie theaters across the country was actually taking place in neighborhoods all over America. In 1991, Los Angeles, CA became ground zero for race-tensions in America, as the brutal beating of African-American motorist Rodney King, by several LAPD police officers, was recorded and aired on national news. A year later, the city would erupt in violence and chaos as the officers who beat King were acquitted of any wrong-doing, and the public –incensed- reacted in anger and frustration.

To make the claim that news coverage in this country is slanted is not to say too much at all. But I feel compelled to point out that the manner in which the 1992 Los Angeles Riots were covered by the mainstream American media, in my opinion, left most observers with two prominent themes; *violence and chaos* in general on the part of young urban *black and brown people*. The overriding images of that event, and the takeaway message that I think most Americans not directly affected by it were left with, was stay away from –or contain at all costs- urban youth, because this is what they're capable of doing to your neighborhood.

Intense and overblown news scrutiny of inner-city violence perpetrated by African-American and Hispanic youth, the prevalence and pervasiveness of the entire gangster genre –in music and film- coupled with the growing mainstream fear of all things urban, led to the passing of new legislation in the form of California's 3 Strikes Law.

....

California's 3 Strike Law

The gist of the law is that there was a perceived notion amongst mainstream society that all too often, criminals were being arrested and released for repetitive, and *violent* crimes. The growing consent was that the criminal justice system had too many loopholes and sentences were too short. The mainstream American media played its role by over-representing and sensationalizing crime statistics in urban communities, fueling a perceived need for more stringent policies and sanctions for repetitive law offenders.

Facts1.com, or Families to Amend California's Three Strikes, is a website that fights for a serious revamp of the law itself. The California law was put into effect in 1994; other states have since enacted similar if not identical measures. Here are just a few interesting factoids concerning the 3 Strike law, from the F.A.C.T.S website (www.facts1.com):

1) 25 years is the mandatory minimum sentence under the 3-strikes law for a third strike
2) In California alone, there are approximately **3,629** individuals who have received at least a 25-year to life sentence for **nonviolent** (usually drug-related) offenses.
3) **23,511 to 162,000**, represents the change in California's prison population from **1980** to the year **2000**
4) **45** and **26** represent the percentage of African-Americans and Hispanics receiving third strike sentences based on the total number of third strike recipients
5) African-Americans in Los Angeles county have been charged under the 3 strikes law **17 times more** than Whites.
6) **21** and **1** represent the number of prisons and colleges / universities built in California since 1984.
7) California, one of –if not the- richest states in the nation, **ranks 41st** in educational spending per student.

....

In the pop-culture world, towards the end of the gangster rap era -a genre which has never completely died out, but which has instead steadily morphed and adapted throughout the years– a young, brash, and brilliant music mogul in the making by the name of Sean "Puffy" Combs, and his music label Bad Boy Records, would burst upon the scene behind the success of the company's main attraction, the Notorious B.I.G., or Biggie as he would come to be known. Another young talent by the name of Tupac Shakur was also on the rise in the early 90's, and at first, the two rappers were close. However, through a tumultuous series of events which included several members of the rappers respective cliques, as well as the non-fatal shooting of Tupac outside of a New York recording studio, the rappers would eventually become bitter rivals, and the focal points of a media motivated East Coast / West Coast musical war.

As Tupac moved west and aligned himself with the infamous -if not aptly titled- Death Row Records, things quickly got out of hand. And in 1996, on the ever-visible and intensely illuminated Las Vegas strip, Tupac Shakur was gunned down. Almost six months later, in March of 1997, Christopher Wallace, otherwise known as the Notorious B.I.G., was gunned down in Los Angeles, CA, while leaving a music industry after-party.

While the still unsolved mysteries surrounding the deaths of the two rappers continue to fuel barber-shop arguments, talk show fodder, books, DVD's, and silver screen smash hits, the fact remains that although their deaths were untimely and tragic, sad and unforgivable, they were no different than the many unsolved murders of young promising and talented black men; they simply garnered more attention. Their deaths were not assassinations, as some have asserted, and as the media would have one believe, they were simply homicides.

The distinction is an important one to make, because the words garner a measurable difference of impact upon a given community. The relevance and effect of an assassination can be felt in the halt of a social movement, in the demise of political or ideological ideals or an idealist, in the loss of momentum for a given cause. Heads of state are assassinated, political leaders are assassinated, Malcolm and Martin were assassinated. Tupac Shakur and Christopher Wallace were murdered. The distinction is important to make because the mainstream American media did everything in its power to present these two young rappers as Martyrs for the entire African-American community!

The danger in this is that if these two young men were martyrs, then what exactly were the ideals and beliefs that they died for? What was their ever-lasting message to the African-American and wider community? What lessons do our youth take away from their lives? The answers to those questions are where the dangers lie in the pervasiveness and persistence of the American media system and its fascination and glorification of ghetto living and thug life; in the propaganda of hip-hop-culture.

....

The Big Picture

Operation Desert Storm

i. In response to the Iraqi invasion of Kuwait (August 2, 1990), and more so in response to Kuwait's proximity to Saudi Arabia and its oil, the U.S. responded by economically sanctioning and blockading the Saddam Hussein led regime.

ii. On January 17, 1991 the U.S. lead coalition of the United Nations began its air attack.

iii. The U.S. dropped over 60,000 tons of bombs within a month and a half timeframe.

iv. While that figure may sound large, it is substantially smaller than the figure of most prior U.S. engagements

v. Primarily an air assault operation, ground troops were able to subdue the Iraqi army with ease, and the skirmish was declared over on the morning of February 28, 1991.

Apartheid

i. The word "apartheid" actually translates to "apartness" in Afrikaans, the unofficial language of the people of South Africa.

ii. It is a social policy of color-stratification, much like the United States Jim Crow Laws of the post slavery era – although much more stringent- which had existed in South Africa since the beginning of white settlement in the country; around 1652.

iii. Formalized and systematized into law in 1948, with the succession of the Afrikaner Nationalist Party.

iv. Would stay a legalized social system until 1994, when the country's constitution was rewritten, the first democratic elections were held, and Nelson Mandela was elected the first black President of the country.

....

Chapter 8

The New Millennium: Dazed and Confused

"In the ghettos that the (system) has built for us, the (system) has forced us not to aspire to greater things, but to view everyday living as survival – and in that kind of a community, survival is what is respected."

- Malcolm X, from the Autobiography of Malcolm X

For the better part of the past decade, the African-American community has been stuck in a downward spiral. At present, we have no collective voice, or at least, it doesn't feel as though we do. If anything, the unifying images and messages of the African-American community have been rims, grills, "getting money", or the all encompassing Hip-Hop culture. A small percentage -but significant amount- of our athletes keep getting into trouble, and the positive things that the rest of them do with their incredible salaries never make the news. There seem to only be a handful of working African-American female actresses; because we seem to see the same rotation of them in Hollywood films. And at the time that I began writing this book, Barack Obama was still an unknown to most, and rapper Hurricane Chris' song "A Bay Bay" was a national hit –other notable songs of the time were E-40's "Go Dumb", Soulja Boy's "Yaaah!", "Chicken Noodle Soup", and DJ Khalid's "I'm So Hood".

The current situation of the African-American community is one in which entertainment has become 'reality' for a generation overexposed to the media. A generation primed for Attention Deficit Disorder by an over-the-top, gotta-have-it-now, instant gratification, go-for-self-no-matter-the-consequences media system. We find ourselves lost; lost in society's re-presentation of ourselves. Young Black people have become living breathing caricatures of themselves. We are no longer a concern of the system because we have lost ourselves within the system. The media now defines what Black is; and the more ignorant and violent the subject matter, the more "Black" it is.

Probably the biggest blow to any positive movement amongst the African-American community in the last 10 years, in my opinion, has been the emergence of the Hip-Hop persona "50 Cent"; a living, breathing, Tony Montana. And again, I hold nothing personal against Curtis Jackson – A man provides for himself and his family the best way he knows how. Curtis Jackson, the man, is an extremely intelligent individual, and a shrewd businessman. But there is a bigger reason than that behind the persona of 50 Cent being forced down our throats through music videos, movies, video games, clothing lines, sneakers, television shows and soft drinks.

Now understand that I bumped "In the Club", "21 Questions", "Magic Stick", and "I Get Money" along with everybody else. I, not literally but figuratively, bought into the hype as well. Curtis Jackson has made, and continues to make major mainstream hits! But the emergence of 50 Cent -a brash young hustler who defied death, survived the drug game, and became one of the best selling rap artists of his generation- has given the mainstream American media system the perfect opportunity to redefine what it is to be *Black*. Or, more to the point, it has let them redefine for our youth what it means to be a 'real Black man'; you have to be hard, you have to be violent, and you have to be willing to *get rich or die trying*. The glorification of ghetto has taken on a new and more insidious turn over the last decade. And the significant difference in today's messaging, versus the messaging of the previous two decades, is that the weight in negative or violent images versus positive or inspirational images and messages has shifted drastically; creating a serious imbalance towards the negative.

Let us quickly glance at the home entertainment and gaming industry for example. Within the last decade or so, a sinister development has begun to take shape in the video gaming world. Greed has once again infiltrated the corporate war rooms in which decision-makers decide choices which affect the masses. Game-makers have seemingly lost all connection to any sense of morality or social accountability; and apparently, anything goes in pursuit of the all mighty dollar. The question 'what can we make?' has resoundingly trumped any reservations regarding whether or not *we should* make it. We've gone from Pac-Man and Star Wars, from Mike Tyson's Punchout, Super Techmo Bowl and Street Fighter, to the Grand Theft Auto series. And while racing and sports games, such as Midnight Run and the annual John Madden Football installations are wildly popular, graphically violent and socially irresponsible games such as Saint's Row and Grand Theft Auto I, II, and III -where game players can impersonate street toughs and gangsters as they not only work on their hand-eye coordination, but also desensitize themselves to and improve upon their own criminal instincts- are even more successful.

This situation raises several questions. The first of which is who is it that these games are geared towards and marketed to, and why? What are the moral and societal ramifications of these games upon their audience? And more importantly, why do these games sell out faster than any others?

There is a serious problem at hand when a society becomes so cannibalistic, so greedy and materialistically hungry, that it begins to feed upon the weakest and most indefensible parts of itself. The *thug life* fascination began in the 80's and carried on throughout the 90's, has taken a new form in the 2000's; in the shape of digital gangsters remote controlled by children. This is a very scary predicament on a number of different levels, but mainly with respect to the effects of desensitization and acceptance.

On one level, these games work to desensitize those who would be the most likely victims or perpetrators of such violence – young minority and poor people – to the realities that they face. On the other hand, it desensitizes those most likely to be unaffected by such violence – middle and upper-class youth – to the realities which they may very well never face. In so doing, there is again the separation of "us" and "them"; the passive acceptance of a "that is how they live", and an "it's not exploitation if it's true" type of mentality. A mindset like that reinforces a privileged class fear of the underprivileged and poor.

And that fear is not unfounded. These games are emboldening. In these so called 'games' you can steal cars, purchase prostitutes, rob retail establishments, shoot, kill, and maim anyone whom you choose, including law enforcement authorities. You can actually cause so much mayhem that the Army is sent out to try and stop you; and stopping you means killing you – ending your life. But of course in the games, all one need do is hit the restart button, and he or she can be right back at it in no time. I am a grown man, but I can remember playing these games in college for hours on end, at the conclusion of which I was left with a very vague and playful air about me that, even if half-jokingly, believed that I could probably pull some of those things off. And I was in my early twenties! Imagine the effects of playing a game like this for the same time period, or even for five minutes, on the mind and psyche of a child. We must remember that the old "You can be anything you want to be" adage works the other way as well; it's not solely tied to positive aspirations.

As Malcolm X told Alex Haley in his autobiography, "What makes the ghetto hustler yet more dangerous is his 'glamour' image to the school-dropout youth in the ghetto. These ghetto teenagers see the hell caught by their parents struggling to get somewhere, or see that they have given up struggling in the prejudiced, intolerant white man's world. The ghetto teenagers make up their own minds they would rather be like the hustlers whom they see dressed sharp and flashing money and displaying no respect for anybody or anything. So the ghetto youth become attracted to the hustler worlds of dope, thievery, prostitution, and general crime and immorality... Thicker each year in these ghettoes is the kind of teenager that I was – with the wrong kinds of heroes, and the wrong kinds of influences." (Haley, Alex. The Autobiography of Malcolm X. p. 359) Malcolm may have spoken those words some forty years ago, but still they ring true.

The American socioeconomic system, via the media, promotes ignorance in minority groups by highlighting and celebrating those individuals that convey ignorance. The *system*, being the convoluted convergence of private and public entities (government agencies and international conglomerates), does this because ignorance and stupidity serve to do nothing more than stifle our minds and immobilize our bodies - unless of course we are being coerced to mindlessly consume without question, or intimate and then imitate the ignorance we view. We are all 'going dumb' and it is profitable for only a select few – and even they aren't who you think they are.

So how do we fight a system that has been designed from the beginning to produce such an outcome? One part of the multi-layered answer is leadership. It is easy to understand how the underserved masses have come to exist in our present situation when you consider the shift in minority leadership, and most apparently, the shift in mainstream African-American representation over the past few decades; we've gone from Martin and Malcom, to Diddy, 50 Cent, Jordan, Jay-Z, Kobe, LeBron, and the Grammy Award winning (seriously) 3-Six Mafia. As historical and groundbreaking as his presence may be, President Obama's impact upon America and more specifically the African-American community, has been -without a doubt incredibly positive, but also- very short-lived. Since the late 1960's, with the loss of Malcolm and Martin, musicians and athletes have become the most recognizable - and more importantly – most influential figures in African-American representation. The system has done a great job of discrediting and disgracing our elders such as Al Sharpton and Jessie Jackson. But even they have not always stepped up to the plate, so to speak. The very entertainment industry which we give so much of our support and efforts to mocks us by *awarding* African-American actors and musicians only when they portray our oldest and most degrading stereotypes.

Denzel Washington, for example, is arguably one of the greatest actors of this or any other Hollywood generation. The man could be handed the Oscar for virtually any role he has ever played. He brought Malcolm back to life in Spike Lee's "X". He brought theatres to tears in John Q. Yet the only role he has taken home the aforementioned and most coveted acting recognition for, is that of a dirty, murderous cop in the movie Training Day. "King Kong ain't got shit on me!", indeed. For all intents and purposes in the memories of America, Halle Berry became the first African-

American woman to receive the Oscar for her part in a gratuitous and raunchy sex scene with none other than Billy Bob Thornton (no disrespect intended to either actor). For me, the last straw was broken when musical act Three Six Mafia became the first rap group to be awarded an Oscar *(an Oscar!!!)* for their role in the production of the 2005 movie Hustle & Flow's hit song "It's Hard out here for a pimp".

Now for those of you sucking your teeth and proclaiming me a hater, and believe me I can already here the words forming in your thoughts, let me just say that pointing out the obvious is not hating. Pointing out the fact that Denzel Washington has performed at Oscar level for most of his career, in everything from character pieces to Shakespeare reprisals, but was only rewarded for his efforts after he embodied every possible negative and damaging stereotype regarding African-American men, is not hating – it's insulting! It's insulting that Halle Barry, an incredibly beautiful, successful, and extremely talented Black woman, received her hardware for a role in which she played to a couple of age-old generalizations and stereotypes concerning African-American women as being the bedrock of a broken family and being overly-sexualized. And I quite honestly don't even know what to make of the 3-Six Mafia situation, other than to ask a simple question. Can you honestly explain to me how, in the history of Black music, 3 Six Mafia becomes the first African-American musical *group* to win an Oscar?!? (Isaac Hayes won in 1971 for Shaft) Can anyone explain this with a straight face? I could almost hear the Academy, or whoever it is that makes these Oscar decisions, laughing and snickering in their million dollar penthouses and offices, like, "they want recognition? We'll give them recognition for everything we think they are, and they'll be happy about it!" … *Brilliant!*

And while the mainstream media celebrates everything ignorant in the African-American community, academics like

Cornel West, Bell Hooks, Asa Hilliard III, Minister Michael Eric Dyson, and Dr. Calvin Mackee speak the truth to the people, but because they do so they receive little to no publicity; their message falls upon the ears of a select few. To turn a common phrase, they preach to the choir. When our elders do find the courage to speak the truth to our community, like Bill Cosby, we recoil in disgust and scream, *how dare you?! How dare you air out our dirty laundry? How dare you not accuse someone else for our misfortunes?* Although, with all due respect to Bill, when someone's pants have been not only pulled down, but nailed to the ground for several centuries, it is quite difficult for that person to be able to pull them up by him or herself – let alone be able to find the bootstraps on which they may begin to tug. But I get the gist of what Bill was saying, as I'm sure most of us -once we get past our own pride and stubbornness- do. I guess it's true what they say though, people really don't like to be told about themselves, no matter who they are.

The purpose of this book is to awaken us all from the malaise of our educational system, shed illumination upon the invisible guiding hand which has steered most of us into our present realities, shake us free from the stranglehold of the American media system, and make us aware of and able to break loose from the mental shackles and excuses we employ in rationalizing our own condition. The media is the most powerful opiate known to man, and its grasp has most of us either too *high* to mobilize against it, or too afraid to question it. We must introduce Media Studies and Media Literacy, as well as ethnocentric studies, into our most elementary levels of teaching. We must be true to ourselves, and once again depend on ourselves -and the strength of unity found within our community- to better our situation; because *we can rely on no one else to do this!* Our children, and all children for that matter, need help translating, reconceptualizing, and understanding the world that is being presented to them 24 hours a day, 7 days a week, 365 days a year.

....

The Big Picture

September 11, 2001

- In the early morning hours of September 11, 2001, four commercial airliner jets were hijacked.
- At 8:45am American Airlines Flight 11 crashed into the north tower of the World Trade Center.
- At 9:03am United Airlines Flight 175 crashed into the south tower of the World Trade Center.
- At 9:43am American Airlines Flight 77 crashed into the Pentagon
- At 10:10am United Airlines Flight 93 crashed in Somerset County, Pennsylvania; the attempted hijacking of which, apparently went wrong.
- Osama Bin Laden and the Taliban are widely suspected as the culprits of the attacks.
- 26 days after September 11th, the U.S. launched a staggering air attack on Afghanistan, and the "War on Terror" had begun.
- Shortly thereafter, President George W. Bush, Jr. called for the invasion of Iraq on the basis of the country's possession of Weapons of Mass Destruction.
- No W.M.D.'s were ever located, but Saddam Hussein was captured, and eventually executed.
- U.S. forces remain in Iraq to this day…

Hurricane Katrina 2005

- In early 2005 the National Weather Service predicts that 2005 will be the worst year for hurricanes in the country's history.
- Wednesday, August 24, brings the first alert of a tropical storm forming in the Caribbean. Many areas of the Gulf Coast begin preparing for a possible Hurricane, but many individuals opt to "stick it out", and are set on staying put.
- Before making landfall in the early morning hours of Monday, August 29, Hurricane Katrina becomes a category 5 (the strongest possible rating) storm with winds in excess of 175m.p.h.
  - Levees begin to fail as early as 7a.m. that morning.
- Civil unrest breaks out in areas across New Orleans and in some parishes Martial Law is declared.
- The Superdome and New Orleans Convention Center become shelter for tens of thousands of displaced individuals.
  - Conditions in the overcrowded buildings are described as "hellish", as reports of rape, violence, death, and neglect are constant in the media.
- The Federal Emergency Management Agency, or FEMA's first response teams don't reach New Orleans until 5 days after Hurricane Katrina made landfall. In comparison, it took the agency 1 day to respond to the 2004 Tsunami in Indonesia.
- Hurricane Katrina is officially the costliest weather related disaster to ever hit the United States.
  - Katrina's impact was felt monetarily, in loss of life, and socioeconomically, as the event raised many questions and brought several issues to the forefront of American consciousness, regarding race and class in this country.

- Four years later, many of the communities devastated by Hurricane Katrina are still in shambles, and remain uninhabited.

....

Chapter 9

Crisis Point

According to the U.S. Census Bureau information for the year 2006:

The African-American population is nearly 14% of the total US population, at 38.3 million; 18.2 million males, and 20.1 females.

*The Caucasian / White population is upwards of 65% of the total US pop.
*The Hispanic / Latino population is nearly 15% of the total US pop.
*There are nearly 13 million Asians in America according to the 2006 Census information.

From a story found on The Black Collegian entitled "Demographic profile of African-Americans; 1971 to 2001", by Nicholas A. Jones and James S. Jackson – info sourced from the U.S. Census Bureau 2000:

"While we have increased in number, the majority of the African-American population continues to live in the South (54%). About 19% of African-Americans live in the Northeast, as well as the Midwest (19%). Only 8% live in the West. These regional proportions have stayed virtually the same over the last 3 decades... Most African-Americans (53%) also continue to live inside the central cities of metropolitan areas. But this is down from 1970, when the black population base in central cities was 60%."

"About half (48%) of all African-American families today are married-couple families, a decline from 68% in 1970. Most other African-American families (44%) (are) maintained by women."

From the Wall Street Journal Online, July 19, 2008. "The End of White Flight", by Connor Dougherty:

"Between 2000 and 2006, eight of the 50 largest cities, including Boston, Seattle, and San Francisco, saw the proportion of whites increase, according to Census figures. The previous decade only three cities saw increases... If the current trends continue, Washington and Atlanta (both of which currently have black majorities) will in the next decade see African-Americans fall below 50% for the first time in about a half-century."

"San Francisco has lost so many African-Americans that mayor Gavin Newsome created an 'African-American Out-Migration Task Force and Advisory Committee' to help retain black residents... In S.F., African-American deaths now outnumber births."

This information comes from a 2005 article entitled "African Americans in Higher Education: Now for the Good News", found in _The Journal of Blacks in Higher Education_

• A new report from the U.S. Department of Education states that in 2002, the latest year for which complete data is available, there were 1,950,905 black students enrolled in higher education in the United States. This is the highest level of enrollments for African Americans in history.

• In 2004, 17.6 percent of all African Americans over the age of 25 held a four-year college degree. This figure has increased significantly from 13.8 percent in 1996 and 11.3 percent in 1990.

• Older blacks are heavily enrolled in college. According to a report from the U.S. Census Bureau, 8.8 percent of the black population over the age of 18 was enrolled in higher education. In contrast, only 7.5 percent of all whites over the age of 18 were enrolled in higher education. This advantage in favor of blacks is due to the large number of older blacks who enroll in college. For the 30-to-34 age bracket, 8.4 percent of the total African-American population is enrolled in college. For whites, the figure is 6.6 percent. For adults over the age of 35, 2.5 percent of all blacks are enrolled in college compared to 1.7 percent of whites.

• A 2005 report from the Association of Governing Boards of Universities and Colleges found that blacks are 13.6 percent of all trustees at public universities and 7.6 percent of all board of trustee members at private institutions. All told, blacks hold 4,400, or 8.8 percent, of the approximately 50,000 trustee positions in American higher education.

A quote from a July 17, 2008 San Francisco Chronicle story entitled "24% Likely to drop out at State's High Schools", by Nanette Asimov: (Figures come from the California Dept of Education)

"Nearly 1 in 4 California students will drop out during high school, state educators said Wednesday, basing their prediction on what they said is the most accurate information about student attendance they've ever collected... The new statewide report shows that 351,035 students in the class of 2007 earned a diploma, or 68%."

*Some counties in California have a drop out rate at or above 40%

     I realize that I have yet to inform you, the reader, of what it is exactly that I do for a living. I've hinted at it throughout our conversation by mentioning that I work in higher education, but I've never given away my title or position. To be quite honest with you, my candidness was intentional. All too often I've found that people form judgments based on titles and status, and not on content or character –not that I claim to have an exorbitant amount of either. My secrecy was intentional -because I don't really think that it matters what my profession is. Quite honestly, it doesn't matter to me what yours is either. I didn't write this book as one professional to another. I wrote it as one concerned American citizen to another; as one African-American male to the African-American community, as a son to a father or mother, brother or sister, niece or nephew, as a friend to another friend, or perfect stranger. I wrote it because I care.

I have spent the last 5 years of my life working in the field of Higher Education as an Admissions Counselor; an Assistant Director of Undergraduate Admissions to be exact. I've worked at two different institutions, the first of which I graduated from, the second being my current employer. I am proud to say that I have not only enjoyed my time spent at each, but have also gained a tremendous amount of experience from both. I have logged countless hours on the road, given hundreds of presentations, read thousands of applications, and met with several more thousand students and families. I truly do enjoy my job.

I wrote this book because of my time spent in this job. I wrote it because of the path of my life before I began working in this field. And I wrote this book because of the direction I'd like to see this country take after I am long gone from this profession. This book is the direct result of daily and long-term frustrations I've experienced in my short career, in regards to working with and recruiting underrepresented students. Over the years I have noticed some alarming trends forming within the African-American community in particular, and this is my attempt to address them.

Currently there are close to 38 million African-Americans living in the United States; that number grows to upwards of 40 million if you include mixed-race individuals. That number makes us only about 14% of the US population. We are now the second largest minority group in the country next to the ever expanding Hispanic/Latino population, which now sits at upwards of 44 million, or about 15% of the total population.

Demographically, we haven't really moved around all that much in the last half- century. More than half of us still reside in the South (54%), and only 8% have made it out West. A more significant statistic to keep in mind is the fact that more than half of the African-American population (53%) live within inner-city or metropolitan areas. So when you hear the term 'urban' -as in urban-school districts, urban planning, or urban youth- someone is referring to a specific reality for more than half of the Black people in this country.

Now, it is also important to note that more and more African-Americans have begun to move out into suburban areas, which is a good sign because it represents financial and material progress for a good number of Black people. However, in concert with this trickle of outward movement is another somewhat alarming trend, and that is the subtle gentrification and out-pricing of minorities in several major metropolitan areas around the country. And now that term 'gentrification' will spark a furious response from many city planners and politicians who will argue that they are simply moving forward with urban advancement, and catering to upwardly mobile professionals who want the access of living in metropolitan areas. And with that sentiment I would agree completely. But what I would also point out is that the *process* of catering to those individuals is also the process of displacing a significant number socioeconomically challenged individuals -of all ethnicities; individuals that we have all of a sudden decided to cast aside rather than include in the reinvigoration of these areas. We are, in effect, kicking them out of the car instead of bringing them along for the ride!

The underlying issue here is not actually that greedy or racially motivated policy-makers are displacing certain peoples, but that certain peoples who happen to more often than not belong to certain ethnicities and socioeconomic backgrounds aren't keeping up with the pace of progress, and the looming question is why. Why is there this success divide? What are the roots of the problem, and why is it growing over time instead of shrinking? And outside of all of the historical and societal factors, what are the more individual and personal factors that are playing into this situation?

The first place I would look is high school; and the realities for those who finish and those who don't. Now it has been statistically and socially (socioeconomically) proven over time, that an individual is more likely to be financially rewarded in correlation to said individual's level of educational attainment. In short, the more educated a person is, the more that person will be paid over time. As things stand currently, according to the most recent figures from the U.S. Bureau of Labor Statistics, for individuals at least 25 years of age, working full time, the national annual income for someone with no high school diploma is around $20,000. The average annual income for an individual with only a high school diploma is about $30,000. It's close to $50,000 for an individual with a Bachelor's (4yr.) Degree. Do you see a pattern?

Here's where things really get interesting. Let's look at an individual with a Master's Degree. The national average annual income of an individual 25 years or older, working full-time with a Master's Degree, is in the neighborhood of $60,000. Now the national average for a two income household is only a bit above $67,000. So what that means is that nearly half of the individuals with a Master's Degree are able to out earn a two person household by themselves. And now I am not the most mathematically inclined individual, but that makes sense to me. As a matter of fact, it makes dollars and cents.

In order to get a Master's Degree, one first has to attain a Bachelor's degree, and one can only do that by going to college, right? Well let's look at the realities of what college campuses look like these days. There are over 3,500 institutions of higher learning spanned across this great land of opportunity. Those schools range in size from petite Liberal Arts colleges with populations of anywhere from 1,200-5,000 students, all the way to large Public Institutions anywhere from 12,000-65,000 students. The national average for African-American student populations on those campuses is 2%. The national average for Hispanic / Latino students on those campuses is around 6%. The average for Asian students is much higher, but one must take into account that the term 'Asian' is a very broad descriptor; it accounts for all individuals of Indian, Japanese, Chinese, Korean, or Pacific Islander descent –and there are certainly large discrepancies amongst those populations as well. Now as we just covered, the national populations of African-American and Hispanic / Latino peoples in this country are only 14% and 15% respectively, vis-à-vis there are obviously less college age individuals within those ethnicities to be spread amongst the nation's institutions of higher learning -but still!

And those stats do not speak to the fact colleges are actively and earnestly trying to diversify their applicant pools. Both private and public institutions, regardless of whether or not they have the ability to say so legally, are pro-actively searching for qualified underrepresented students of all ethnicities and demographics; the problem is that the number of qualified applicants is sharply decreasing rather than increasing –the supply is not keeping up with the demand. And the problem is not solely the fault of the students themselves, but of the educational and societal realities they are facing.

One of the main issues of today is that the k-12 curriculum is no longer *speaking* to the students. There is a growing disconnect between the relevance of the material that students must cover on a daily basis, and the understanding of how said material will one day prove useful to the student. In many ways the public educational system is set-up in a way that facilitates the short-sightedness of the student; the end goals are so distant and the paths to those goals are equally confusing. For many students, myself included, the idea of becoming a doctor or a lawyer, an Engineer, or Financial Planner –while it sounds nice- is so foreign, so unattainable, that it becomes a pipe dream. And so it is easy for a student to revert back to the professions or goals that he or she does understand –that he or she is familiar with, or at least, that they see as an actual and realistic possibility. And if you just so happen to be a person of color, then the most readily available images and messages of what you can actually attain are very prevalent in the mainstream media; in the form of athletics, entertainment, or crime.

One of the more puzzling developments of the last few years, that I've noticed at least, is that this is not only the case for poor or underprivileged students of color. There is a growing trend of well-to-do minority students from well-to-do schools situated in well-to-do communities, that aren't doing all that well. It's almost infuriating to me when I see an African-American student, coming from a very educated family, with all the resources one could possibly ask for at their disposal, barely getting by academically, or worse. Just this year for example, I reviewed the application of a young African-American student whose parents both had professional degrees. The student attended a high priced *hoity-toity* private school in Southern California, and the overall application read as if neither the student nor the family wanted for anything they could not attain. The student however, was a 'C' student at best. His test scores were in the tank. His courses were some of the most basic offered at his high school. And do you know what his essay was about? It detailed his aspirations of becoming a music producer.

Now, he may end up becoming the next Sean "P. Diddy" Combs, and that's all fine and well. I don't have a problem with that. But what I do take issue with is a media system that is so loaded with specific and limited examples of minority achievement and success, that this obviously capable and resourceful young man, has decided to throw all of his eggs into an incredibly small basket. And he is not alone.

Sometimes it feels as though today's students -and even more alarming- a growing number of adults, have completely forgotten about the past. They have either actively or unknowingly chosen to neglect or disrespect the struggles of our ancestors. They have turned their backs on Martin, Malcolm, Douglas and DuBios. They have tuned out the screams of those lynched and burned. They are indifferent to the strength, pride, and perseverance of those who came before them. Again, it is my opinion that the African-American community is no longer a threat to or concern of the system, because for the most part, it has lost itself within the system.

Something else to consider...

According to the U.S. Department of Justice: Bureau of Justice Statistics

On June 30, 2007 —

– 2,299,116 prisoners were held in federal or state prisons or in local jails – an increase of 1.8% from year end 2006
– 1,528,041 sentenced prisoners were under state or federal jurisdiction.
– There were an estimated 509 sentenced prisoners per 100,000 U.S. residents – up from 501 at yearend 2006.
– The number of women under the jurisdiction of state or federal prison authorities increased 2.5% from yearend 2006,

reaching 115,308, and the number of men rose 1.5%, totaling 1,479,726.

At midyear 2007 there were **4,618 black male** sentenced prisoners per 100,000 black males in the United States, compared to **1,747 Hispanic male** sentenced prisoners per 100,000 Hispanic males and **773 white male** sentenced prisoners per 100,000 white males.

- That means that for every **100** black males in the United States **4.6** are in prison
- For every 100 Hispanic / Latino males in the United States 1.7 are in prison
- For every 100 White males in the United States 0.7 are in prison

"82% of inmates in the criminal justice system **are high school dropouts**." (U.S. Bureau of Justice Statistics.)

"A black man is more than six times more likely to be slain (than a white man). The difference is most stark among black men 14 to 24 years old: They were implicated in a quarter of the nation's homicides and accounted for 15% of the homicide victims in 2002, **although they were just 1.2 percent of the population**, according to the Bureau of Justice statistics."

("Being a Black Man"; Washington Post, 2007)

Chapter 10

What I See...

As I mentioned before, part of the duties of a college Admission Counselor, aside from the actual reading of applications, is travel. It's the road warrior aspect of the position; scheduling and attending high school visits and college fairs, receptions and interviews. It is the *recruiting* facet of what we do, a term that leaves some of us with the uncomfortable connotation of a used car salesman. For some, we feel an internal struggle with our altruistic selves which make the argument that we are not merely sales people in search of more customers, more clients, and more applications for our respective organizations. No, we are conduits of information. We are simply conveying the importance of education and offering our institution as a single option in a vast sea of possibilities. But truth be told, we are both things at once, whether we like it or not.

Travel is a part of the job, and it's a fun part. It can be exciting, it can be rewarding, and it can also be extremely frustrating and somewhat disheartening. Frustrating in the sense that when you step away from the ivory tower of any given institution, or when you leave the confines of a pristine and well manicured college campus, you hit the ground running from high school to high school, from fair to fair, and from the top to the bottom of the socioeconomic totem pole. You can go from a world of privilege to a world of poverty and inequity in a matter of minutes, or a span of city blocks. And for those of us who truly care, it can be a bit of an emotional roller coaster.

It's always pleasant when you visit the nice schools in the nice parts of town. The drive to these schools can be calming and even sometimes breathtakingly scenic. The surrounding neighborhoods are usually quiet and well kept, and there is usually an abounding air of optimism, of opportunity, of bigger and better things to come. The students you see at these schools are the same students you see on your own campus, visiting with parents in tow - or more often than not, with their parents towing them. They are usually in the midst of a multi-college road trip, with your campus either at the exciting beginning, in the malcontent middle, or at the exhausted end of said trip. They don't really ask questions, either because they're quite familiar with mom and dad's stories about the good times they had while attending college X, or the tales of their coworkers son's or daughter's experience at this school or that, or simply because at this point they just don't care anymore. They're bored, and as a byproduct that makes them boring.

Sometimes though, it can be the other extreme. Students can sometimes be so amped up, so polished, so programmed, that it can leave you with an unsettling feeling – as if you'd like to grab them and shake them free of the mold they've been poured into. Anyone who's watched collegiate cheerleading will understand where I'm coming from. When and if these students at these schools do have questions, they usually deal with study abroad programs, internships, undergraduate research opportunities, graduate programs, or job-placement rates – all good questions, and the types of questions you wish every student knew to ask.

I don't necessarily consider that aspect of the job as being all that rewarding personally. Sure it's fun, it's engaging, and it's an invigorating creative process involved in the soft sell of any given institution. Why should students with so many options choose your school over another? Why should they travel this distance and pay this much money, when they can stay at home and go to the college down the street? That is the daily challenge of life in the world of college admissions; as miniscule as it may seem.

But now the fun part, the truly rewarding facet of the position, is when you have a hand in making things "click" for a student – that intangible but monumental moment when a student finally gets it, and begins to realize their true potential and the options in front of them. While I wish it were not the case, these proud moments are usually few and far between for most of us in this field. They usually come during special presentations to special groups which are brought onto your campus by non-profit outreach organizations. In short, it's the opportunities you have to help guide a young, intelligent, and questioning mind –which more often than not belongs to a student of color– that help to shape and inspire most of us in this profession. These moments are so special for us because they hit very close to home, especially for those of us who were the first in our family to go to and graduate from college.

The opportunity to demystify the experience and process of getting to college is something that I personally take much joy in. When you are the first in your family to go to college, or when you are the oldest sibling, or even more so when you are the first generation of your family born in this country, there are a multitude of pressures heaped upon your shoulders - both knowingly and unknowingly – by yourself and your family. From day one, the message you receive is, "Go to school, get good grades, go to college, get a job." For so long this mantra is driven into your daily routine that after awhile the reasoning behind it begins to fade. And when that happens, the practice of going to school becomes a very hum-drum process; something you do because you have to, a task you complete on autopilot. And more often than not, when you are the child of immigrant parents, your educational choices are steered towards particular occupational fields that you may not even have an interest in – important sounding positions such as doctor, lawyer, and engineer.

I take delight in throwing that steering off course, in spicing up the hum-drum, in reviving the educational experience for students. The educational process is about much more than the grades you receive, the school you get into, or the job you get afterwards. It's also about the people you meet along the way, the experiences you have, the memories that can never be taken away, and the new information and opportunities that you stumble upon. It's about the network you create, and the skills you develop. It's about the indescribable feeling of pride and accomplishment that courses through you as you walk across that stage, shake that hand, and receive that piece of paper that signifies the completion of a journey – the conclusion of a chapter in your life, but the beginning of a whole new story. I get a certain pep in my step when I have these kinds of interactions with students. I feel re-energized and recharged, and it's a natural high that I can ride for weeks.

However, in the admissions field, the downside of that high comes with the realization that in most cases, you actually only have a single "touch-point" with any given student. The reality is that we meet, present to, and converse with thousands of students each year, and the best we can do is hope that we make each interaction as memorable as possible for that particular student. However, the plain and simple truth is that sometimes it's just not possible. Sometimes your time is too short, or the distractions too great, for your message to truly have an impact.

Visits to impoverished and resource starved schools can have a downright depressing affect on me personally. Although I am always able to hide my despair behind a strong and undeterred upbeat disposition, inside I feel the turmoil of anger and disgust at the conditions these students must deal with. Be it overcrowded schools, dilapidated buildings, dated textbooks, inundated counselors, stressed-out teachers, or the impossibly heavy burden of serious life issues, these are tensions you can feel on these campuses – especially if you once dealt with similar circumstances. Those tensions become tangible in the lack of self-confidence that students express. They become real through the students acceptance of the mainstream stereotypes about them. And they become dangerous when the students begin to feel that there is nothing positive they can do to change them.

Those days and those visits are the toughest for the admission counselor, not so much for the students. The students are numb to their situation – they live it – it's their reality. But to the high-minded admission counselor who comes in upbeat and triumphant, positive and purposeful, those days and those visits can have a dampening effect on one's outlook. I compare it to the experience of an immersion trip participant – the altruistic do-gooder who comes away from their experience questioning, yet unable to measure the amount of impact they truly had.

I find balance on those days by remembering my stance, my mantra, or better yet my guiding philosophy since day one in this profession –which has always been that if I am able to arm you with as much knowledge as I possibly can surrounding the circumstances and realities of your current situation, as well as offer you insight into any possible means by which you may be able to improve your situation and overcome the obstacles facing you, then the rest folks, is on you. As the saying goes, you can lead a horse to water, but you cannot make him drink. My hope is that through this conversation, we can begin to lead this nation to water - because I believe that deep down most of us are dying of thirst.

They say you are what you eat, but these days we are what we watch, and what we listen to; what the *experts* in the media say we should be. If we are not careful we will all run the risk of becoming caricatures of ourselves; simple puppets whose strings are controlled by an intangible but very real puppet-master.

The simple fact of the matter is that this nation is only forty years removed from one of the most tumultuous and defining decades in its history. While it is undeniable that society, technology, and medicine have made tremendous strides within that time span, it would be ludicrous to think or even suggest that we've cured all of society's ails in that short time period – Barack Obama or not!

The most immediate solution to our situation is knowledge. Knowledge of history. Knowledge of self. Knowledge of capitalism. Knowledge of conglomerates and their subsidiaries. Knowledge of marketing strategies. Knowledge of the media, and most importantly, knowledge of its system. I like to believe that people do certain things and develop certain routines because they know of no other or better way to go about accomplishing their goals. That said, we as parents and grandparents, as mentors and counselors, older brothers and sisters - and even as students ourselves – cannot leave the responsibility of this education, or the attainment of this knowledge, up to the schools alone.

As is the case for most public schools, especially those in urban areas, the educational facilities find themselves overrun, underfunded, and outdated. They are in need of as much help as we can possibly offer. And so the journey of educational attainment must begin with the individual in search of it.

Chapter 11

Bringing it All Together

The zeitgeist of American culture is one which has evolved over several centuries and through a shift a several *isms*. In the beginning, we existed in an openly racist and oppressive society, masked under the pretense of equality and freedom. In an attempt to rid ourselves of the tyrannical order of European rule, pilgrims – North America's first immigrants - voyaged across the Atlantic and began to supplant and displace this country's original peoples, the Native Americans. As our populations increased and we needed more land to sustain our families and our economy, we began to branch out in all directions. We still had ties to the old country through economy and industry, and so we exported our labor to the imported slaves.

We built this great nation upon the blood, sweat, and tears of Black, Red, and Brown-skinned peoples, while the White or *"fairer"*-skinned peoples enjoyed the egalitarian ideals of the newly minted Constitution. Even after the official system of slavery and indentured servantry had long since dissipated, the unofficial social caste system which persisted in maintaining a brutally racist American reality for those of non-European descent was never resolved.

Although the country's demographics would alter dramatically over the next several generations, the social atmosphere would remain stagnant. It would take a series of devastating and seemingly debilitating events –race riots, lynching, the disfigurement of a 14 year old boy- before the negroes of this country would be spurred into action through social and political activism. Malcolm and Martin would evoke the spirits of Garvey, Douglas, and DuBios in galvanizing the oppressed and bringing their causes to the forefront of the American consciousness. Their courage and persistence coupled with their untimely and violent deaths would inspire a generation of black people to stand up to degradation and inequality. And although their legacies continue to live on, the organizations which strove to follow in their footsteps would be undermined by the veiled actions of a deeply embedded "good-old boy" American government.

Soon, the very real, and simultaneously embellished threat of Communism would shift the mainstream consciousness away from the concerns of inequality at home and towards a war in Vietnam. Vietnam itself would present the perfect opportunity for the cryptocracy of the American government, "whoever these invisibles are that control this complex uncontrollable country", to unleash a new form of oppression upon the country's underprivileged; in the form of Heroin. While inner-city communities reeled from the physical and social implications of the war, they also struggled to survive the devastating onslaught of America's newest import.

It was at this point in our timeline that Hollywood saw fit to provide the American public -and eventually the world- with a new definition of African-American cool. Pimps, playas, prostitutes and drug-dealers became the poster children for inner-city Black life. In the 1970's in general, society's youth checked out. The steady progression from Marijuana, to Acid and LSD, and then on to Heroin had finally taken its toll. As the world's superpowers vied for supremacy, American society tried its best to deal with addiction. Well, at least that could be said for most of White America. For as the American government tirelessly tried to impress its will –its democracy- upon the peoples of Central and South America, as well as the peoples of the Middle East, it found a new form of funding for all of its many U.S. trained and supported guerilla rebellions; the importation of cocaine and munitions sales to American ghettoes –those ever expendable communities.

In concert with the surmounting pressure from outside forces, the 1970's would mark the beginning of the self-imposed downfall of the African-American community as a whole. The levy that we had held strong for generations upon generations, against outside forces and pressures, began to burst at the seams; and soon many of us found our heads below the watermark. With no apparent leadership and a subsequent lack of direction we began to fall prey to the negative images and messages that we had always been able to resist. We became complacent to look to and rely upon outside forces -namely the government and its welfare program- to create financial stability in our homes. With no national voice to dissuade us against the ever present danger of blindly following the media, our youth began to look outside our homes in search of role models and hero figures. For the next three decades, and on into the turn of the new millennium, the majority of our communities would begin to unravel themselves through drugs, violence, and fiscal irresponsibility.

But before all of that, in the 1980's, while the explosion of gang activity, crime, and death rates soared to never before seen heights in many urban communities, a biased and government friendly Media System did very little to question the *how* and the *why* of the developing situation. How had these illegal narcotics which are not native to the neighborhoods of Compton, Brooklyn, inner-city Philadelphia, Chicago, or Miami, ever even gotten there? How had these military-grade guns and ammunitions -which are also not manufactured in Black communities- all of a sudden found themselves within these communities in such abundant supply? No, those questions were not asked, or at least they were not focused upon. Oh, but the *who* and the *what* of the situation– young black males and violence- were crucified and scrutinized in the American news media day in and day out. When the true journalists felt compelled to ask the real questions and attack the actual issues they often found themselves the recipient of much resistance, ostracized, or without a job. The way the media presented it, the situation was merely a matter of Environmental Determinism; these people lived this way and did these things because that is the way of life in the ghetto- so heed our warning and stay away. Let them kill each other one by one and eventually we won't have to deal with the problem anymore.

And in the 1990's, the entertainment industry once again found its calling in portraying only the most base and reprehensible aspects of the African-American experience. Year after year, movie after movie, and song after song not only depicted but celebrated gangs, violence, sex, drugs, and any other form of escapism that would enthrall the minds of young urban youth and keep them pre-occupied with all of the wrong things. As Hollywood and the Music Industry deflected criticism by explaining that they were only catering to a wanting public, no one ever stopped to recognize the fact that limited options leave one with limited choices. If gangster rap was representative of nearly three quarters of the music options that the African-American community had to listen to in order to hear music that was even remotely related to its experiences, then it's not very hard to imagine the genre of music the community patronized most. And if the same can be said about the movie selection produced by Hollywood –a continual theme- on a year in and year out basis (like clockwork!), then it's not that difficult to understand the types of films and images that African-American audiences could relate to.

Once the major players in the American media system realized how profitable the Gangster genre really was, not only within urban communities necessarily, but within suburban and predominantly white neighborhoods (amongst white children), they began to crank up the volume. Pretty soon outraged White America was up in arms and making enough noise to force local and even federal level policy-makers to take notice. Within no time at all legislation had been passed and Gangster Rap found itself the subject of a court subpoena. And in the court of public opinion, a jury of Gangster Rap's *peers* found it guilty of tainting the purity of middle and upper-class America; censorship would be the new law of the land.

And now things really began to hit a little closer to home for the entire African-American community. You see, somewhere between the late 1970's and the turn of the new millennium, the media had successfully found a way to characterize the whole lot of us as a people to be feared; especially young black men. Typecast indeed. And in response to public fears, public policy-makers sought more stringent legislation in an effort to thwart the criminal tendencies of inner-city and urban youth; take California's 3 Strikes Law for example.

For the past decade the Media has had its way with the psyche of not only the African-American community, but with most of the American public –especially those of us who do not control the Top 5% of this nation's wealth. The not-so-subtle convergence of public and private entities has created a web of influence so strong, yet so discrete, that most of society is unable to even recognize its own entanglement. The media has effectively turned the musical genre of Hip-Hop into a synonym for *Blackness*; and in turn we as African-Americans -especially our youth- have fallen into the thought process that in order to be Black we must fully embrace our *Hip-Hopness*. Mainstream America beware; for these days the psychological attacks and subtle mental manipulations are not only aimed at minorities and inner-city youth. In suburbia, you'll find that the media has essentially turned Paris Hilton and Britney Spears into the Superheroes of White Womanhood; truly great role models for all young ladies to aspire to! And we wonder why our little boys and girls are not only more sexually aware, but more sexually active at increasingly younger ages.

This is not to say that we as a society have played no role in our own demise. We are just as guilty as any greedy CEO or power hungry politician for falling prey to - and not challenging- the traps that have been set for us. We fell for the media mind games which fueled the fires of an East Coast vs. West Coast Hip-Hop grudge match. We bought right into it when the media portrayed the deaths of two *rappers* –albeit two of the most passionate and charismatic artists we have ever produced- as if we had lost the martyrs of some new age Civil Rights Movement. Tupac Shakur and Christopher Wallace's deaths were homicides; not assassinations!

It was the African-American community who was awestruck by the narcissistic and materialistic styling of the "Bling-Bling" era. We fell for that – that's our fault! Instead of saving or investing our money, instead of building wealth, we collectively decided that as soon as we had the means to do so we were going to let everyone within eyesight know that we had money too! That we were ballers! That we were important. Like Kanye West said, " Let's take 'em back to the club / Least about an hour I would stand on line / I just wanted to dance / I went to Jacob an hour after I got my advance / I just wanted to shine" (Kanye West. "Touch the Sky") And Kanye wasn't the only one. The Bling-Bling era was fun. It was care free. It was carpe diem incarnate. When Lil'Wayne, BG, and the Cash Money Boys broke on the scene we were all fascinated with getting our shine on. But once again, somewhere in there we lost ourselves and forgot to remember that it was just entertainment. We made the mistake of internalizing Bling-Bling into our identity as a people. And the rest of the country laughed at us. Hell, I'm at fault here too. I've "made it rain" one day and scraped together change for lunch the next. *Always the trend-setters, rarely the profiteers of the trends.*

Now make no mistake about it, a lot of the images and themes present in Hip-Hop are representative of the realities that most African-Americans in this country have shared or had to deal with at some point in time in our lives. Bling-Bling has been around since the early 70's, since Mr. T, Run DMC, and LL Cool J. Drugs, violence, and crime have been realities in our communities since before we could remember, and we've dealt with all of it at our own pace, and on our own terms. More than that, the tradition of adorning oneself with jewels and riches in an attempt to display one's social or material status, has been with us since our ancestors. The problem came when we lost control of our own identities –when corporate America stepped in and began to repackage and re-create our own image and sell it back to us and the rest of the world in the form of music videos, CD's, movies, video games, magazines, etc. The corporately sponsored bombardment of "gangsterism" upon the increasingly impressionable youth of the country has finally taken its toll; embedding itself into the very fabric of young ethnic mentality. And now we have a very dangerous situation on our hands.

But, maybe I'm wrong. Maybe there is no secret alliance between the government and the media to conspire against minorities? Maybe there is no unwritten pact linking government policy and media programming? Perhaps the only true connection between slavery, racial propaganda, Jim Crow and the Black Codes, red-lining policies, Cointelpro, blackspoitation films,

Ghetto genre films, negative news coverage, and the marketing of urban – is simple economics?

There is the possibility that that is the only connection. But that stance would need the base assumption that all of those things exist, or existed, in a vacuum; completely independent of each other, and that they existed solely for the benefit of the American economy. One would have to back the argument that American society's only benefit from slavery was the profit it gained from the cotton trade, or that racial propaganda and Jim Crow and Black Code laws were propagated to maintain or improve the economic standards of living for the general American society – and that those things had no negative effect on peoples of African descent economically, socially, or psychologically. One would have to make the argument that red-lining policies were instituted by banks and lenders solely because they represented sound financial decisions, and in no way disadvantaged a particular segment of American society. The argument would need to be made that Blackspoitation films, the Ghetto film genre, and the unbalanced media coverage prevalent in this society since day one, have all been sound capitalist responses to the realities of this country. And more importantly, one would have to make the case for all of this with a straight face.

Chapter 12

A New Hope... President Barack Obama

November 4, 2008, the United States of America witnessed history. On that day, Illinois Senator Barack Obama became President-Elect Barack Obama. On that day history was made as the popular vote of this country had for the first time in its two hundred and thirty-two year existence elected an African-American President. November 4 was the culmination of a long and exhausting, and exhilarating political season that captured the hearts and minds of this country like none other before it. Although Arizona senator John McCain's presidential aspirations were stifled that night, he graciously and gracefully accepted defeat while also offering his best wishes and hopes to the new leadership and to the country. Perhaps for the first time in the entirety of the presidential race, we were allowed to see the more candid –more human- side of McCain. While his campaign may have often veered towards the negative and derogatory –not so subtly playing upon negative racial and religious stereotypes- even he could not ignore the significance of the moment.

With the election of Barack Obama as our next Commander In Chief, America regained its credibility. And more so than that, we got a little bit of our swagger back as well. A campaign founded upon the audacity of hope, inspired millions and millions of Americans to once again believe in the possibilities that can be realized in this great country. As the cameras scanned the crowd of

Barack supporters in Chicago's Grant Park, a tearful Jesse Jackson, an elated Oprah, and countless other faces of any and every ethnicity and background gave testament to the fact that although this country has often stumbled, and has sometimes fallen, we will always get back up, we will always charge forward, and perhaps for the first time in this nations history we may all begin to do so together. It was a poignant and powerful reminder that not too long ago people marched for this, people sat in for this, people were beaten, burned and lynched for this, and two of our greatest leaders were assassinated for having the audacity to give us hope for this. It was as monumental a moment as I have ever experienced in my lifetime.

The election of Barack Obama comes at a perilous time in this country's journey; a time of fear and uncertainty, of danger and excitement. His presence restores a much needed credibility that had been lost in the midst of a befuddled and misguided eight year stint in Washington with George W. Bush, Jr. at the helm. It gives the rest of the world optimism that America may now actually begin to practice the democracy it has always preached. It cannot be overlooked that an unimaginable number of the world's citizens celebrated and rejoiced along with Americans on November fourth.

But as President-Elect Obama stated in his celebratory speech, "This is your victory. And I know you didn't just do this to win an election. And I know you didn't do it for me. You did it because you understand the enormity of the task that lies ahead. For even as we celebrate tonight, we know the challenges that tomorrow will bring are the greatest of our lifetime – two wars, a planet in peril, the worst financial crisis in a century", and a community at a crisis point. Oh yes, even though we have come so far in a relatively short amount of time - even though the last forty years have proven to be some of the most progressive we have ever seen - not all of us have progressed at the same pace, and in fact, many of us have been left behind altogether. Although this moment in time is not one that we can afford to waste languishing over the divisions amongst us, it is the perfect opportunity to recognize and address them. It is the perfect time for our leaders and our elders to right the wrongs that have disadvantaged entire populations and generations of peoples. It is the exact moment when our youth must find the courage within themselves to once again believe in themselves and the things that they are capable of achieving. If Barack Obama teaches us nothing more during his presidency, he has already taught us enough. Through his actions, through his persistence, and simply by his presence, he has shown us that if we really want to, if we honestly and earnestly dedicate ourselves to achieving and attaining a particular goal, then yes, we can!

Chapter 13

Moving Forward

A Serious Re-evaluation of our K-12 Education is needed

"Our schools have been scientifically designed to prevent over-education from happening. The average American (should be) content with their humble role in life."

- William T. Harris, U.S. Commissioner of Education in the late 1800's

One of the biggest problems I have with our current educational system, is that it seems, to me at least, to be short-sighted, and ass-backwards. We look at the lack of African-American students in AP and Honors classes, we look at the math and science achievement gap, we look at standardized test scores, and we wonder why? Why are little black children so far behind in these areas?

I've always believed that you cannot change an equation by looking at its end result. In order to have an effect on the outcome of any given situation, you need to have some sort of influence over the variables which produced it. We need to open our classroom, living room, and lecture hall discussions up to the topic of our media system and the devastating impact it's having upon our youth. The popularity of the movie American Gangster (2007), as well as the identically titled BET documentary series which chronicles the rags to riches stories of infamous gangsters, has more to do with the fact that African-American students aren't doing well in school than the idea that they just aren't good at it. The 50 Cent phenomenon has more to do with the fact that there aren't many of our students in AP and Honors classes, than the concept that the work's just too hard. Our children are too busy attempting to get rich or die trying, rather than get smart by spending time studying. We need to step outside of the traditional education system thought box and really begin to tinker with the equation. The question is not one of aptitude, it's one of application. It's one of interest, and it's one of relevance.

According to Sheldon Richman, editor of The Freeman, a periodical produced by the Foundation for Economic Education out of Irvington, New York, and author of Separating School and State, "Public schools are intended to create complacent 'good citizens' – not independent thinkers – because political leaders don't like boat-rockers who question things too closely." (Sheldon Richman. Separating School and State: How to liberate America's families; Future of Freedom Foundation: Fairfax, Virginia. 1994) It is this inherent contradiction in the importance and value of an education that we as a society must challenge.

We must challenge the educational system steeped in schooling and as opposed to educating; giving structure without giving agency. I use the term agency here, to mean that we should be arming our students with *a means of exerting power or influence* (Random House Dictionary); of empowering them with the ability to create action and take control of their lives. For the vast majority of our students, the current public school educational system fails miserably at this. To me, the differences between schooling and educating can be seen in the employment of fill in the blank or multiple choice questions, over open-ended, thought-provoking essay responses. In the utilization of worksheets over dialogue. In the concentration of efforts towards test preparation over mastery of material. These are the differences in schooling as opposed to educating. One gives a student rudimentary building blocks for run of the mill productivity. The other empowers the individual to question and challenge, thrive and grow. Schooling trains and conditions the mind, while educating stimulates the soul!

We must improve our Public School Funding

We need a grassroots campaign to increase the funding of our public schools that is widely publicized and national in scope; something akin to GQ Magazine's Gentleman's Fund, The Gap's (RED) campaign, Lance Armstrong's Yellow bracelets, or even the Pink Ribbon campaign to promote support of breast cancer research. I propose a blanket Non Profit Organization which focuses on the accumulation and distribution of the wealth and generosity of the individuals that our children already admire and look up to.

If we created a nation-wide organization which organized and distributed the charitable giving of a community's, or region's most successful individuals (i.e., athletes, entertainers, entrepreneurs, etc.) to that community's, or region's most in need public schools, we could create a funding windfall for the schools which lack funding altogether.

With the combination of the NBA, NFL, and MLB alone for example, there are several hundred African-American and Hispanic and Latino professional athletes, each with considerable annual incomes well in the neighborhood of $200,000 or more. If we could organize the contribution of merely a small percentage of that, we could, in the big picture, contribute quite a bit to the funding of our struggling public schools. This would entail a tremendous pooling of private resources, as well as a detailed and overarching audit system for which to ensure accountability, but the end result would be the benefit of the public school system. This organization of giving would not only include professional athletes or entertainers, but any successful and willing individuals able to contribute.

On one end schools would receive far more funding than what would come to them based solely upon their local and state property taxes, and on the other, the donors would enjoy favorable tax donation benefits, as well as much needed and tremendously positive public relations. As I see it, it's a win-win situation not only for the recipients, but also for the donors.

We must engage in Media Studies

I believe that Media Studies should be introduced into the most elementary levels of education in this country, and continued on throughout high school; college curricula is specific enough for a student to designate their own educational path. We have spent enough time educating our youth about George Washington and the "founding fathers". We see daily, and have experienced all throughout history, what the U.S. Constitution has done for us, and in particular for the African-American and minority populations of this country. We need to start preparing our students to be able to better cope with the images they see and the messages they hear. We need our young people to become media literate, and we need it to happen now.

And why not study the media? It studies you! The producers of media employ psychologists, anthropologists, sociologists and economists to try and figure you out. They use focus groups, surveys, and street teams to discover what the latest trends are so that they can be the first to market those trends to you. Matter of fact, they've gotten so good at it that now they attempt to create trends and give you the impression that you came up with the idea (*Astroturfing).

They know how you roll! The "urban market" is the most likely to liquidate its income on accessories and leisurely activities – we make the least and spend the most, and the media system celebrates us for it! Buy, buy buy! Spend, spend, spend! Consume, consume, consume! We are a multibillion dollar economy unto ourselves -but most of us don't see a dime from it, and our communities don't see a cent. Continue to play the game if you want. But I, for one, am in search of a better way.

And so you may be asking, how do I bring Media Studies into the classroom, and into my everyday life? Most universities have a website dedicated to Media Studies. There are over 3,500 institutions of higher learning in the country, and I'm willing to bet money that you live in a state that has at least one. That said, contact the Media Studies, Social Studies, Sociology, Political Science, or Communications Department of that university and see what resources or references they are able to offer you or your students.

Here are a few solid Media Studies and generally solid educational websites that I've found just by searching the World Wide Web:

Action Coalition for Media Education – ACME –

www.acmecoalition.org

Media Studies.com

www.mediastudies.com

Society for Cinema and Media Studies –

www.cmstudies.org

Young African-Americans Against Media Stereotypes (YAAAMS)

www.yaaams.org

Facing History and Ourselves

www.facinghistory.org

For Your Information

Just thought you might like to know which Media Giants control virtually everything we hear and see from the media: nearly all television channels, movie production companies, radio stations, and news outlets are run through these entities:

AOL Time Warner

3 Production Studios including: Warner Bros Studios, New Line Cinema and Fine Line Features, several television networks including; WB Television Network, HBO, Cinemax, Time Warner, Comedy Central, CNN, TBS, TNT, Cartoon Network, Turner Classic Movies, six book publishers, 3 sports franchises, and several magazines including; Time, Life, Fortune, Sports Illustrated, Money, People, and Entertainment Weekly, to name a few

Viacom

MTV, BET, Nickelodeon, VH1, CBS, CW (formerly UPN), Paramount Theaters, Blockbuster Video, seven book publishers

Disney

The Disney Channel, ABC, ESPN, A&E, The History Channel, Lifetime, 6 Film Production Companies including: Miramax Films, Touchstone Pictures, Walt Disney Pictures, four book publishers, 8 theme parks

Rupert Murdoch's News Corporation

Owns the Fox family of networks, 20th Century Fox Studios, Fox Searchlight Pictures, six book publishers, 5 professional sports teams, and has partial ownership of 3 major sports stadiums, and 3 newspapers

Bertelsmann

Owns 8 publishing houses, 9 record labels; including RCA and Bad Boy Records

Sony

19 record labels including; Columbia Records, several production and distribution houses; Sony Pictures, Columbia TriStar Pictures, and video game giant Playstation

Vivendi

MCA Records, Polygram, Island / Def Jam, Motown, Universal Records, Universal Studios, USA Networks

We must stop supporting and start challenging an unbalanced and biased Media System

How can you begin to recognize and challenge the mechanics of the American media system? You can begin by questioning everything you see and hear in the Media! Here's where the old saying "Believe half of what you see, and even less of what you hear", comes into play. Remember that the status quo is profitable for a lot of people, and that most of the things you hear and see in the daily media probably, in some way or another, go along with maintaining the status quo.

Do your own research. Don't take anyone's word for it. In my experience, the people who think they know it all are the ones who truly know the least; they're also the most likely to be frighteningly judgmental, and annoyingly –if not dangerously- opinionated! It's a funny paradox, but the more educated one becomes, the more one realizes that there is a ton of information out there that they don't know. Probably the worst thing that a growing mind can do is take someone else's word as the all-knowing truth on any given subject.

There are a lot of things out in the world that are objective, such as 2 plus 2 is four, and unless there is a major mathematical revolution sometime in the future, that will always be the case. There are also an infinite amount of subjects that are, and will always be, subjective: such as good versus evil, right versus wrong, one man's hero versus another man's villain. Do your own homework on a subject, and formulate your own informed opinion. Remember, every study has a hypothesis that it is either trying to prove or disprove; all research has an agenda. If history teaches us anything, do not let "common sense" be the sense that you employ when forming opinions regarding a person, place, religion, or thing.

Remember that Media Representation is unbalanced for a reason, and that reason is probably not beneficial for you. Enjoy entertainment, but don't forget that it's simply entertainment. As has been said for generations, everything's fine in moderation. It's completely fine, and most definitely normal, to enjoy movies, music, television shows, magazines, and video games of all sorts from time to time. Or more to the point, it's perfectly normal to consume mass media. The problem comes when one consumes so much of it that he or she begins to lose themselves within it. Always remember who you are!

Beat the odds, break the stereotypes, and create your own reality! The way the media portrays things, one would believe that there are far more African-American males in prison than there are present on college campuses throughout the nation. But that has never been the case! According to the Bureau of Justice Statistics, as of 2005, for African-Americans 18-55 years of age, there were 801,995 individuals incarcerated in jail or prison. For that same age group, there were 864,500 individuals attending an institution of higher education. For the age group of 18-24, what most people falsely consider as the average college-going age range (only about 25% of all college students fall within that age range), there were 106,000 African-American males incarcerated, and 473,000 attending school; nearly a 4:1 ratio. ("What Black Men Think"; which uses figures from the United States Bureau of Justice Statistics, for the year 2005)

The reality is that there are numerous falsehoods, stereotypes, and negative generalizations attached to nearly every ethnic group walking the planet. And depending on a variety of factors -age, ethnicity, sex, culture, religion, location, etc- you might have more or less of those harmful stigmas attached to the group or groups that you most readily identify with. The task then becomes one in which you must carve your own path, and create your own identity. You must not waste precious time and energy in the fruitless pursuit of changing people's opinions about you. You must only concentrate on being the best and most productive individual that you can be for yourself, and for those that care about you; your family and your community.

And last but not least, we must once again regain our Pride and Purpose

One of the main reasons I began this project was that I had reached a point of frustration within my field of work, but also with society as a whole. I had visited enough schools, spoken to enough groups, watched enough television, seen enough movies, attended enough conferences, and observed enough minority children mindlessly going through the motions of education, that it had begun to bother me deeply. I had paid attention to, and secretly monitored, the subtle collusion of Hip-Hop and "Blackness" being put forth by the American media monster, and I slowly came to the realization that our cultural melting pot had reached a boiling point. The media inspired -urban youth absorbed- infatuation with everything gangster and ghetto had pierced the core of African-American and Hispanic and Latino identity, and I felt as though our children had become unsuspecting and unquestioning drones of American pop-culture.

The product of quasi-Muslim, but unquestionably ethnocentric and somewhat militant grandparents on my mother's side, I harkened back to the overarching themes and messages of blackness in the 1950's and 60's; the call for civil liberties, the demand for respect within and for the community, and the perilous environment which made those things a necessity. I looked back upon those times, I considered our current situation, and I honestly felt as though something had been lost in the translation. Something had been lost along the way. Some piece of that time period, and without question a large sum of that momentum, had not carried its way to the present. I feel as though a large part of the disconnect between that time period and today comes from the fact that people do not feel as though our current conditions are as perilous as they once were. And with respect to the severity of the danger inherent in our daily lives, those people are undoubtedly right, but when looking at the socioeconomic realities that the majority of us face, things have only marginally progressed in comparison.

And so I began on this journey, and what I found was that that momentum, and that vision, that unity and sense of urgency, had not been haphazardly lost along the way, but had in fact been forcibly taken away! Our leadership had been struck down, our communities dismantled, our sense of self reconstituted, repackaged, and sold back to us. We had lost ourselves within the American Media System. We knew not where to look for answers, we knew not who to turn to for direction, we knew not what to stand for, and so we fell for anything.

But still I remained hopeful, for what I also saw when I looked at Black America -at the African-American community- was our genius; our beauty, our grace, our ingenuity and resolve! Our genius is beautiful because it cannot be overstated or overestimated. It cannot be qualified or quantified. It is intangible. Some might argue that it is as innate to us as the melanin in our skin. I would offer that it comes from something deeper than that, some unspeakable spark within, some indiscernible bond between all peoples who have come from and through an origin of oppression. There is a strength which has been deified. A swagger which is idolized. (*No one on the planet got swagger like us!*) A presence which is both villainized and glorified. But for whatever that ungraspable thing is, it is unknown. And that lack of understanding is enough to spark both fear and amazement in all who encounter it -sometimes simultaneously.

We are living in a time of hope and uncertainty, fear and possibility. No one truly knows what lies ahead for this great land of opportunity, be it economically, domestically, internationally, or socially. But we do know one unquestionable and empowering truth, a galvanizing and edifying reality, and that is that we are still here! We are still here after 400 plus years of slavery! We are still here after one Civil and two World Wars! We are still here after a Holocaust! We are still here after a Great Depression and several subsequent recessions! We are still here after two atomic bombs, the Civil Rights, and Vietnam! We are still here after September 11. We have weathered the waters of Ike, Rita, and Katrina. We've made it through the Bush! Folks, we can make it through anything!

This is America, and we are Americans, and we should all be proud of that. But if the last decade of American existence has taught us anything, there is indeed something to be valued and appreciated in the display of humility. The world is becoming smaller and smaller by the minute, and with each and every technological advancement. We must all do our part to become better neighbors with our international brothers and sisters. We must no longer boast that 'We are number one!' For starters, that's just not good sportsmanship –and more than that, since when did the human race become an actual race? Secondly, just how assured can we be when making that assessment these days? No, from now on we should carry ourselves with a quiet confidence, an open mind, and a caring heart. Believe me, we'll make more friends that way.

For my community in particular, the African-American community, we must find ourselves within the murk of the American Media System, as well as in our own consciousness', and reclaim our own identity. We must look within, and be truthful to ourselves; owning up to and accepting all aspects of ourselves. We must allow no one but us to define us, for we are the indefinable! We are the popper, the poet, the philosopher and the professional, the pusher and the preacher! We are Jay-Z, 50 Cent, Tupac and Biggie! We are Common, Mos Def, Dead Prez, and Nas! We are Chappelle, Pryor, and Murphy! We are Jill Scott, Badu, Arie, and Keys! We are Saul Williams, Black Ice, Black

Thought, Talaam Acey, and Simmons! We are Chestnutt, Diggs, Washington, Lee, and Latifah! We are Cosby, Condoleeza, Colin Powell, and Jackson! We are Oprah and Bob Johnson! Jordan, Kobe, and Lebron too. We are Oscar Grant! We are Obama! We are African-American. We come in all shapes, sizes, colors and shades. There is no singular definition of our blackness, because our blackness is whatever we want it to be.

And for our students, the question is no longer one of aptitude. It is no longer one of ability. It is no longer a question of whether or not our students *can* do what is necessary to bridge the achievement gap, but whether or not they *will* do what is necessary. The question is now one of application; one of accountability. Will our students take it upon themselves to be self-motivated, goal-oriented individuals, or will they allow themselves to fall prey to harmful stereotypes and generalizations which aim to snuff out their bright and promising futures? Will we support them and guide them in their struggle, or will we stand idly by and let them flounder? My friends, my family, my fellow countrymen, no other questions are as important at this time, and in this moment; for it is we who hold the keys to our success -it is we who must achieve.

Yes we can!.. Yes we must!.. Yes we will!

The Beginning

199

"I've had enough of someone else's propaganda... I'm for truth, no matter who tells it. I'm for justice, no matter who it is for or against. I'm a human being first and foremost, and as such I'm for whoever and whatever benefits humanity as a whole."

- Malcolm X

201

BIBLIOGRAPHY

Hilliard, Asa G.; Martin, Luisa. "The Education of African People; Contemporary Imperatives". Black Child Journal. Cited June 2007

Fields, Barbara J. *Race-The Power of an Illusion*: California Newsreel. 2003

U.S. Census Bureau, "Table 3: Annual Estimates of the Population by Sex, Race and Hispanic or Latino Origin for the United States: April 1, 2000 to July 1, 2006"; Release date: May 17, 2007

Hughes, Michael; Kroehler, Carolyn; Vander Zanden, James. Sociology: The Core. McGraw Hill. 2002

Marshall, Gordon. A Dictionary of Sociology. Oxford University Press. 1998

Kenneth, Terrell."*Virginia School Tops America's Best High Schools List*": U.S. News and World Report. December 5, 2008

Juliet B. Schor. Born to Buy; Scribner. 2004, p.215

Staff. Being a Black Man. Washington Post: 2007

Senator Barack Obama. "A More Perfect Union"; Delivered Tuesday, March 18, 2008. Philadelphia, PA

"Slavery". The Columbia Encyclopedia: Sixth Edition. Columbia University Press, 2008

"Scientists unearth early skeleton". BBC News: March, 7, 2005. Cited June 3, 2008

"NOVA: This Old Pyramid". Aired on KTEH-PBS on August, 1, 2006; Cited June 3, 2008 at www.PBS.org

Hilliard, Asa G., III."What Do We Need To Know Now?". Winter 1999

Lincoln, Abraham; Douglas, Stephen; Nicolay, John G.; Hay, John, ed. *'Fourth Joint Debate at Charleston, Illinois, September 18, 1858' in 'The Complete Works of Abraham Lincoln, v. 4'* . New York: Francis D. Tandy Company, 1894

"Civil War". The Columbia Encylopedia; 6th Edition. Cited 2008

McElrath, Jessica. "The Freedman's Bureau": About.com; 2007, cited 6/5/08

Wormser, Richard. "Ku Klux Klan: The Rise and Fall of Jim Crow". Educational Broadcasting Corporation, 2002

Steelwater, Eliza. The Hangman's Knot: Westview Press; Boulder, CO, 2003

Gibson, Robert. "The Negro Holocaust": Yale-New Haven Teachers Institute; vol. 2, 1979

Pendergraft, Rachel. "What is 33/6": Cited from The Official Website of The Knights Party, USA., at www.kkk.bz, June 5, 2008

"The Great Migration". In Motion: the African-American Migration Experience. The Schomberg Center for Research in Black Culture: cited June 18, 2008

Hillier, Amy (2002), "Redlining in Philadelphia," in Anne K. Knowles, editor, Past Time, Past Place: GIS for History (Redlands, CA: Environmental Systems Research Institute)

Huie, William Braford. "The Shocking Story of Approved Killing in Mississippi". Look Magazine. January, 24,1956. p.46-50

Little, Malcolm "X"; Haley, Alex. The Autobiography of Malcolm X. The Random House Publishing Group: New York, 1973

Washington, James Melvin. I Have A Dream: Harper Collins Publishers. New York, N.Y., 1992

COINTELPRO- Black Nationalist Hate Groups (1967-1971). Church Committee Reports: Book II: Intelligence Activities and the Rights of Americans. Washington D.C., April 26, 1976

Cleaver, Eldridge. Eldrige Cleaver: Post-Prison Writings and Speeches. A Ramparts Book: Random House, NY, 1969

Barsamian, David; McCoy, Alfred. "An interview with Alfred McCoy"; Conducted at the University of Wisconsin-Madison. Feb 17, 1990

Morton, Janks. "What Black Men Think". Iyago Entertainment Group, 2007

"Vietnam Era Draft Classifications". The American War Library. Figures obtained from the Vietnam War Memorial; accessed July 17, 2008

Kiyosaki, Robert; Lechter, Sharon. Rich Dad, Poor Dad. Warner Books, 2000

"Sound and Fury over Taxes". Time Magazine. Monday, June 19, 1978

Webb, Gary. "America's 'crack' plague has roots in Nicaragua War". San Jose Mercury News, August 18, 1996

Kornbluh, Peter. "The Oliver North File: His diaries, email, and memos on the Kerry Report, Contras and drugs". The National Security Archive; produced by George Washington University, Feb 26, 2004

Parry, Robert. "America's debt to Gary Webb": The Consortium for Independent Journalism, December 13, 2004

Select Committee Final Report; Book 3: Supplementary detailed staff reports on intelligence activities and the rights of Americans. April 23, 1976, p.24-25

Dowbenko, Uri. "Dirty Secret: Drug Czar Walters and the Iran-Contra Connection". Conspiracy Digest. 2001

Morse, David. "Muticultural America: Redfining the Mainstream". New American Deminsions, LLC., Presented to the Cabletelevision Advertising Bureau (CAB) Conference, Chicago, IL, May 24, 2005

"Understanding the Urban Consumer". Greenfield Consulting Group, Presented to the Advertising Research Foundation, February 7, 2008

Aide, Kate. "1989: Massacre in Tiananmen Square". British Broadcasting Corporation, June 4, 1989

"HIV/AIDS". The Center for Disease Control. Last modified Sept. 3, 2008. Information cited February 16, 2009

Jones, Nicholas A; Jackson, James S. "Demographic profile of African-Americans; 1971 to 2001". The Black Collegian, April 2001

Dougherty, Connor. "The End of White Flight". The Wall Street Journal, July 19, 2008

"African Americans in Higher Education: Now for the Good News". The Journal of Blacks in Higher Education, 2005

Asimov, Nanette. "24% Likely to drop out at State's High Schools". San Francisco Chronicle, July 17, 2008: (Figures come from the California Dept of Education)

Bonczar, Thomas P.; Beck, Allen J. "Lifetime Liklihood of Going to State or Federal Prison". U.S. Department of Justice: Bureau of Justice Statistics, March 1997

Richman, Sheldon. "Separating School and State: How to liberate America's families". Future of Freedom Foundation: Fairfax, Virginia. 1994

Families to Amend California's Three Strikes (FACTS); information cited February 17, 2009 from www.facts1.com

Daniels, Roger. "The Immigration Act of 1965". America.gov: April 3, 2008

Rushkoff, Douglass; Goodman, Barak; Dretzin, Rachel. "Frontline Program: The Merchants of Cool". WGBH Educational Foundation. Aired 2/27/2001 on PBS

Statutes at Large, First Congress; Session II, Chapter 3, p. 103-104. 1790

Rage Against The Machine. "Rage Against The Machine: Killing in the Name of". 1992

West, Kanye. "Late Registration: Touch the Sky". Roc-A-Fella Records. 2005

Dictionaries and Encyclopedias Cited

- The American Heritage Dictionary
  - Internalization
  - Propaganda

- Merriam-Webster's Online Dictionary
  - Black
  - Oppression
  - Systematic
  - White

- Random House
  - Agency

- Wikipedia
  - Astroturfing
  - Cryptocracy
  - Guerilla Marketing
  - Media Literacy
  - Viral Marketing

- U.S. History Encyclopedia
  - Welfare System